NOTES FOR AMERICAN AND AUSTRALIAN USERS

In America the 8-fl oz measuring cup is used. In Australia metric measures are now used in conjunction with the standard 250-ml measuring cup. The Imperial pint, used in Britain and Australia, is 20 fl oz, while the American pint is 16 fl oz. It is important to remember that the Australian tablespoon differs from both the British and American table-spoons; the table below gives a comparison. The British standard tablespoon, which has been used throughout this book, holds 17.7 ml, the American 14.2 ml, and the Australian 20 ml. A teaspoon holds approximately 5 ml in all three countries.

British	American	Australian
1 teaspoon	1 teaspoon	1 teaspoon
1 tablespoon	1 tablespoon	1 tablespoon
2 tablespoons	3 tablespoons	2 tablespoons
3½ tablespoons	4 tablespoons	3 tablespoons
4 tablespoons	5 tablespoons	3½ tablespoons

AN IMPERIAL/AMERICAN GUIDE TO SOLID AND LIQUID MEASURES

Imperial	American	Imperial	American
Solid Measures		Liquid Measures	
1 lb butter or		¼ pint liquid	⅔ cup liquid
margarine	2 cups	½ pint	1¼ cups
1 lb flour	4 cups	¾ pint	2 cups
1 lb granulated or		1 pint	2½ cups
caster sugar	2 cups	1½ pints	3¾ cups
1 lb icing sugar	3 cups	2 pints	5 cups
8 oz rice	1 cup		(2½ pints)

MEDITERRANEAN COOKING

HILAIRE WALDEN

MEDITERRANEAN COOKING

HILAIRE WALDEN

PHOTOGRAPHY BY JAMES MERRELL

HAMLYN

Notes

Standard level spoon measurements are used in all recipes.

1 tablespoon = **one 15 ml spoon**

1 teaspoon = **one 5 ml spoon**

Both imperial and metric measurements have been given in all recipes.
Use one set of measurements only and not a mixture of both.

Eggs should be **size 3** unless otherwise stated.

Milk should be full fat unless otherwise stated.

Fresh herbs should be used, parsley should be the flat-leaved continental variety.

Ovens should be preheated to the specified temperature – if using a fan assisted oven,
follow manufacturer's instructions for adjusting the time and the temperature.

Acknowledgements

Commissioning Editor: **Nicola Hill**

Art Editors: **Meryl James & Penny Stock**

Editor: **Jo Lethaby**

Production Controller: **Sasha Judelson**

Photographer: **James Merrell**

Home Economist: **Louise Pickford**

Stylist: **Karina Garrick**

First published in Great Britain in 1994 by Hamlyn
an imprint of Reed Consumer Books Limited
Michelin House, 81 Fulham Road, London SW3 6RB
and Auckland, Melbourne, Singapore and Toronto

ISBN 0 600 58435 6

A CIP catalogue record for this book is available from the British Library

Printed in China

Front cover shows: Roast Vegetable Salad (see page 41)
Frontispiece shows clockwise from top right: Italian ricotta, labne, Kefalotiri,
Parmesan, mascarpone, Spanish ricotta, Manchego and centre, mozzarella

CONTENTS

Introduction

Mediterranean cooking is a unique combination of simplicity, abundance and lushness –
and while the food is unpretentious and artless, it is utterly captivating. The dishes exude
vibrancy, life and love. Where else will you find food that glows with such rich colours
and intense flavours, or wafts such sensual aromas. The clever use of interesting
ingredients typical of the region means the cuisine is truly memorable, with its use of the
wonderful locally grown fresh produce, flavoured with fragrant herbs and exotic spices.

According to geographers, hunched, gnarled olive trees mark the boundaries of the Mediterranean zone, but to most people it is a region of azure blue seas, piercingly blue skies, clear bright light, ochre and grey soil, brilliantly whitewashed houses with rose or rusty-gold coloured roofs, beaded curtains at the doors and shutters at the windows. Therefore, the region includes eastern Spain, southern France, Italy, Greece, Turkey, Syria, Israel, Lebanon, Jordan, Egypt, Libya, Tunisia, Algeria and eastern Morocco. Although these countries are so obviously divergent in their peoples, lifestyles, political systems, cultures and religions, they still have an inescapable similarity when it comes to food.

Flavours, ingredients and cooking methods are repeated from country to country. You'll find olive oil, garlic, onions, tomatoes, aubergines, peppers, fruits, plenty of herbs and spices, country breads, fish and poultry, the smoky flavour of charcoal-grilled foods and thick omelette 'cakes', such as frittatas, slowly cooked and packed full of vegetables. Each country also shares the pleasant practice of idly nibbling from inviting displays of small tempting dishes before a meal.

Colourful and varied, Mediterranean cooking is flavoured and scented with anything that will add taste or aroma, from garlic to rose buds. It emanates from the homes of ordinary people, where the best real Mediterranean food is to be found, and is simple and unpretentious. It has a freedom that allows each cook to add his or her own, often secret touches, yet at the same time, it is rooted in tradition and unaffected by fashion or fads.

The people of the Mediterranean attach great importance to food and it is prepared with pleasure and pride for the delight and well-being of family and friends. Eating is a relaxed and sociable occasion because people enjoy food and love to share it; visitors are automatically provided with something to eat or drink.

The average Mediterranean diet has recently been acclaimed for its healthiness. Olive oil is the predominant fat (it is even used on bread instead of butter), while the use of butter and cream is severely limited. Quantities of meat are small, but fish and shellfish are enormously popular. Grains, pulses, bread, herbs, vegetables and fruit are eaten in large quantities. Grilling, roasting and slow simmering are the most popular cooking methods.

The countries of the Mediterranean all have a similar climate: dry hot summers and mild winters, rare but violent rainstorms and strong winds – with slight variations according to latitude, thus similar crops are grown throughout the region. The climate also accounts for a shortage of pasture, so livestock is restricted mainly to sheep, goats, poultry and, where allowed by religion, pigs. Since there is a dearth of cows' milk, cheese, cream and butter, Mediterranean cheeses and yogurts are more commonly made from ewes' and goats' milk, although exceptions are found in central and northern Italy.

Over thousands of years, there has been a tremendous interchange of peoples, religions and customs as a result of colonization, migration, invasion, counter-invasion and trading. It is therefore inevitable that similar dishes will be served in a number of countries. However, there has been so much intermingling of peoples that it is a futile task to try to find the origin, if indeed there is one, for many of them. Dolmades, with variations in both name and ingredients, are found from the Middle East to Greece; Middle Eastern Tarator (page 25) and Greek Skorthalia (page 23) are similar garlic sauces thickened with a purée of nuts, while Spinach with Raisins and Pine Nuts (page 59) is eaten in Spain, Italy and Arab countries. Therefore, where there could be confusion in name or spelling, I have used English names.

Mediterranean Cooking includes a whole range of typical regional recipes. The book begins with a selection of recipes for soups and sauces. All over the Mediterranean, soups tend to be hearty and sustaining, for example, Soupe au Pistou (page 17). In the south of France, this sort of soup plays such a major role in the diet that the evening meal has become known as 'le souper'. Perhaps the most ubiquitous Mediterranean soup, however, is fish soup and every region of every country has its own version. Many originated as fishermen's dishes – cooked on their boats as they made their way back to port or when they came ashore, using the fish which were too small or too insignificant to sell.

Either as an integral part of a dish or served separately, sauces are popular everywhere. Mediterranean cooks do not use flour to thicken their sauces – the thickening agent is more usually ground nuts, breadcrumbs or even mashed potatoes. Many sauces are cold, using oil as the liquid. Pesto (page 23) is often referred to as a sauce, but actually has a soft, light spreadable consistency, and Anchoïde (page 21) and Tapenade (page 23), too, are spreads or pastes. Although perhaps not traditional, puréed mezzes such as Aubergine Dip (page 36), may be served as a sauce with grilled or baked meat or fish, or tossed with pasta.

The serving of tapas, antipasti and mezze is a typically Mediterranean custom. These dishes are usually savoury, mildly sharp with lemon juice or vinegar, piquant with capers or olives, aromatic with herbs or fragrant with spices or garlic. All the dishes are served together for everyone to help themselves to whatever they fancy, when they like. There need not be a grand spread; a few simple items, such as Marinated Olives (page 29), salted fresh whole almonds or slices of Parma ham or jamón serrano (Spanish air-cured ham) will be quite enough, particularly at home.

Recently it has become popular to serve one of these individual dishes alone as a first course, a selection of dishes for a simple lunch or supper, or an even wider choice for parties and buffets. Choose from a colourful selection, with varied tastes and textures, such as purées, crisp raw salads, grilled vegetables, cold dressed beans, or herby marinated cheeses, fish and meats – all accompanied by some of the good fresh bread for which the region is renowned.

Eggs are used extensively around the Mediterranean region, in omelettes and eggahs, tortillas and frittatas – some so substantial that they can be wrapped up and taken off to the fields to feed the farm workers for lunch. Eggs are also popular scrambled with tomatoes and peppers to make Chakchouka (page 46) or Piperade (page 48), or served hard-boiled with mayonnaise, Aïoli or Al-i-oli (page 24). As for cheese, because cattle are scarce throughout the Mediterranean, cheeses are invariably made from ewes', goats' or water buffaloes' milk.

Vegetables bring colour to the Mediterranean markets and diet. Chosen with care and eaten with relish, vegetables play a major part in many dishes, often sufficiently substantial to constitute the main part of the meal, replacing meat dishes altogether. Religious restrictions have also played a part in elevating the role of vegetables. In Christian countries, especially in earlier times, many people abstain from eating meat during the long Lenten fast, as well as on holy days and Fridays. The Greek Orthodox Church also bans meat-eating on certain days. Consequently, cooks have learned how to make the very best of each vegetable to create what is now a rich repertoire of dishes.

When it comes to fish, some of the best in the world can be found in the region. Mediterraneans love their fish fresh and simply cooked, preferably over an open fire with nothing more than fresh herbs, a drizzle of good olive oil and lemon juice to bring out the flavour.

Meat, on the other hand, is at a premium, and so is highly respected and cooked in the most sympathetic and quality-enhancing ways. Climate and religion dictate that lamb is the type of meat most often eaten. Sheep and goats are more common in this region than cattle. Veal is popular, and pork is eaten in Greece, Cyprus and in Italy, but of course is forbidden by the religious laws of Judaism and Islam. Rabbit, hare and, above all, wild boar are prized by the passionate hunters of France and Italy, while domestic rabbits and chickens are raised by householders all over the region.

Pulses, grains and products made from them, such as bread and pasta, all feature prominently in Mediterranean diets. Pulses are a good source of protein, and those such as chickpeas and lentils go into dips, sauces and casseroles. Rice is not usually served plainly boiled. Instead, it is first turned in hot oil then mixed together with herbs, spices, nuts, vegetables, seafood, meats, pulses or other grains. Perhaps the best-known of all these rice dishes is Risotto (page 108), with its different variations.

Pasta is always associated with Italy, but many other Mediterranean countries have their own pastas, such as the Spanish fideos. Wheat is not only the ingredient used for making pasta, but also used in couscous, a type of fine semolina, particularly associated with North Africa but also enjoyed in other Arab countries. Bread is an important staple in the Mediterranean diet and every country has its own repertoire of breads.

Finally, the Middle Eastern sweet tooth is legendary and echoed by that of the Turks and the Greeks. The very sweet recipes for which they are renowned are not eaten at the end of a meal, but served with coffee when entertaining and on special occasions. Mediterranean meals usually end with fresh fruit of which there is a colourful, fragrant and luscious abundance. This does not mean that desserts are never made. They do, however, tend to be simple and homely.

So while there are many local ingredients and recipes common to the different countries bordering the Mediterranean, of course – and thank goodness – each country does have its own special flavours.

Spain, for example, is closer to North Africa and the Middle East than other European countries in its cooking as well as geographically, and uses spices more than herbs – parsley being the only one quite widely used. Provençal dishes are redolent of wild herbs, anchovies, olives, orange peel and especially basil. This herb continues to star throughout Italy, where it is joined by rosemary, tarragon, parsley, sage, thyme and marjoram. In Greece, oregano, dill, parsley, lemon, cinnamon and allspice flavour the cooking, while Turks use dill, parsley, cinnamon and allspice. Throughout the Middle East, parsley and mint are the popular herbs and cumin is a characteristic spice. Egyptian cooks also like cinnamon, while the fiery chilli-based paste, harissa, typifies the cooking of Tunisia and, to a lesser extent, that of Algeria.

When making my recipes, I hope you will follow the ethos of Mediterranean cooks and adjust the flavours and ingredients to your taste or according to availability.

Hilare Walden

EQUIPMENT

Although each country has its own special utensils, there are many that are common to all, and easily available elsewhere. These include a selection of heavy-bottomed frying pans, good quality sharp knives and the cornerstone of so many Mediterranean recipes, at least one pestle and mortar. The end of a rolling pin in a bowl often makes the best alternative, as I have indicated in the relevant recipes.

I have mentioned food processors or blenders only where I think they will do. A vegetable mill with two or more different-sized screens is the best piece of equipment for puréeing soups and vegetables, especially potatoes, removing skins from cooked fruits, such as apples, pears and peaches, and seeds from berries.

Heavy glazed and unglazed earthenware pots and casseroles, such as Spanish cazuelas, which can go in the oven and on the hob and retain the heat well, are favoured for long, slow simmering; where no lid is available, improvise with a tight covering of aluminium foil. Unglazed pots are also reputed to give food a special flavour.

Earthenware pots must be seasoned before use for the first time or they will crack. To do this, half-fill with cold water and a good splash of vinegar, bring slowly to the boil and leave to boil until the liquid has evaporated.

Tin-lined copper is also popular as it has similar heat-retaining properties. Enamelled cast-iron ware offers a cheaper alternative.

SPECIAL EQUIPMENT

These items are used for specific dishes and you may like to have have one or two pieces for added authenticity, but the recipes can be made using other equipment.

Italian kitchens have a special knife for slicing Parmesan cheese (a sharp potato peeler may be used instead), a good cheese grater, a very large saucepan for cooking pasta, and a mezzaluna – a sickle-shaped, doubled-handled blade that is very useful for chopping fresh herbs.

DAUBIERE

A French plump, earthenware pot for cooking casseroles. A daubière has a shallow lid that is filled with cold water or ice so the aromatic steam rising from the casserole quickly condenses and drips on to the meat and vegetables to keep them moist. Daubières are now difficult to find, but a sturdy enamelled cast-iron equivalent, doufeau, can be used quite successfully instead.

MOROCCAN TAGINE

A shallow, round earthenware pot with a tall, conical lid like a Chinese coolie's hat, that can be put on a low heat providing it contains some liquid, and is used for slow-cooked stews. An ordinary heavy casserole will suffice.

BEAN POTS

These have rounded bodies with narrower openings at the top and close-fitting lids. Traditionally, they were nestled in the fire and because of their shape, beans cooked in them lost very little moisture by evaporation.

COUSCOUSSIER

This may be made from unglazed earthenware, tin-lined copper or aluminium and is traditionally used for cooking couscous, but it is not necessary with the pre-cooked grain that is now available. A couscoussier comes in two parts – a lower pot in which the meat or vegetable part of the recipe is cooked, and an upper section with a perforated base to hold the grain. The aromatic steam from the stew permeates through the holes to heat and flavour the grain above.

PAELLA PANS

These are round and made of iron, with two looped handles opposite each other, a flat base of a good thickness, and shallow, sloping sides. They should be wide enough to allow the rice to be cooked in a single layer and proportioned so the water required to cook the rice comes up to the edge of the pan handles. A very large frying pan is second best and only feasible for paellas for a small number of people – a 35 cm (14 inch) pan is adequate for only 3-4 people.

Before using a traditional iron paella pan for the first time, to avoid the first paella having a metallic flavour, wash the pan very well in a mixture of vinegar and fine sand, then rinse it and wash normally in hot, soapy water. Dry thoroughly.

Brushing with a coating of oil between use is often recommended as a preventative measure against rusting, but I prefer to dust the pan with an even covering of flour because if there is a long time lapse before another paella is made, oil may become rancid.

BAKEWARE

For useful bakeware for breads and pizzas, see the information on page 111.

INGREDIENTS

Shops now stock a much wider selection of products. Until a few years ago, items such as couscous were rare except in ethnic shops, but they are now sold even in supermarkets. There are also many more specialist shops. Many of the ingredients, especially in supermarkets, are mass-produced, which inevitably means not of the best quality, but the availability of traditional, good-quality products is widening hearteningly, allowing us to produce dishes that more closely resemble the authentic versions.

When travelling, do buy local produce – cheeses, nuts, pulses, dried fruits, olives, salted anchovies and capers, and whole spices from Middle Eastern and North African souks. They have a stronger flavour than those sold in this country.

ANCHOVIES

I prefer salted whole anchovies rather than fillets canned in oil, as they have a superior flavour. Before using salted anchovies, they should be washed, scaled if necessary, the bones carefully removed and discarded and then dried. If they taste too salty, soak them in milk for about 30 minutes.

BURGHUL

Also called bulgur in Turkey and pourgouri in Greece, this is made from hulled wheat grains, cracked by boiling and then dried. You must rehydrate it before use, either by soaking for about 20 minutes, or by simmering for a couple of minutes. The grains must then be drained and squeezed hard to expel excess moisture. Burghul makes an interesting, foolproof and quick alternative to rice and can be flavoured in the same ways as pilaf-type dishes. Use a fine grained variety for tabbouleh and kibbeh, and a coarse one for pilafs.

CAPERS

Salted capers can be bought around the Mediterranean and in a few specialist shops over here. They have a fresher flavour and better texture than capers packed in brine (the salt easily rinses off).

CHEESE

The range of genuine cheeses rather than 'look-alikes' is widening encouragingly.
Buffalo milk mozzarella – genuine mozzarella is made from water buffaloes' milk and has a more pronounced yet delicate, fresher and more fragrant flavour than the more common cows' milk version. It is also more compact, fairly elastic, whiter and will ooze 'tears' of whey when cut.
Halumi – a firm, white, creamy, mild-flavoured cheese, similar in flavour to feta, but less salty. A favourite cheese in Greece, Cyprus, and Lebanon where it is often flavoured with cumin seeds. In Cyprus ewes' milk is traditionally used.
Kefalotiri – a hard, salty ewes' or goats' milk cheese that is good for grating and cooking. **Parmesan** can be substituted.
Ricotta – made from the whey left after making other cheeses, it should be eaten very fresh when it has a delicate, clean, fresh taste; it quickly develops an acidic bitter edge.

COUSCOUS

Made from semolina that has been ground, moistened and rolled in flour. Most couscous is now pre-cooked and needs only to be moistened and steamed to heat through and separate the grains. Butter is usually rubbed into the couscous to help the grains to separate and to enrich them.

HERBS

With the exception of oregano and rigani, use fresh herbs – they give a truer flavour than dried ones. Even so, the flavour can vary quite considerably, so it is important to taste each batch and adjust the quantity used. It is easy to grow a few plants in window boxes positioned in a sunny spot. Keep freshly cut herbs in 'stay fresh' bags available from health food stores and some supermarkets. Freeze them in small quantities. I have never dried herbs to my satisfaction in a microwave. If fresh herbs are an impossibility, use freeze-dried or frozen herbs rather than dried.
Mint – the most widely used variety is spearmint.
Oregano/Rigani – picked when the flowers are in bud, and then dried. The hot, dry climate of Greece gives them just a little more pungency, so buy in bunches or stripped from the stalk from Greek food shops. Home-grown oregano should be allowed to dry for a few hours before using.
Parsley – use the flat-leaved continental variety.

OLIVE OIL

Credited with playing an important part in the healthiness of the Mediterranean diet, it is excellent for cooking as it can be heated to high temperatures and will seal the outside of food, preventing the oil being absorbed.

There is now a burgeoning range of olive oils of different styles and qualities. The descending order of quality, purity, intensity of flavour and price of the grades are as follows:
Extra virgin oil – from the first pressing of the olives, this has the lowest acidity and the most rounded flavour. Commercially produced extra virgin oils are blended from oils of differing character and quality, and will always taste

the same. Extra-virgin oils from estates, farms and village co-operatives have their own individual characters and, as they are unblended, will vary from year to year in the same way as the best wines.

Virgin oil – results from the second pressing of the olives.
Simple 'olive oil' – or 'pure olive oil' – a blend of virgin olive oil and refined oils obtained by chemical extraction.

Extra virgin oil is used in salads or for when only small quantities of oil are required. Virgin oil is used in salads or more widely in cooking, and simple olive oil for cooking.

Flavours and colours of olive oils from different countries – and even from different areas – vary from delicate and grassy to full, heavy and fruity. Spanish oils tend to be lighter than Italian ones, whereas Greek oils are even heavier, because the olives become very ripe before being picked. Colour is no indication of quality – a rich dark green does not necessarily mean a superior oil, although it is an indication of the strength of flavour. Store olive oil in a cool, dark place, but not in the refrigerator.

OLIVES

If you have visited a Mediterranean food market, you will know that olives come in many different varieties and colours; cured in brine, packed in oil, or flavoured with herbs, spices and lemon. Colour differences are linked to ripeness – a progression from green, through yellow or greeny brown, to red, violet, then purple and black. Olives sold loose in barrels are generally of a more reliable quality.

PEPPERS

Charring the skin produces a magical transformation in the flavour of the flesh. Char peppers over a hot barbecue, or halve, flatten and place under a preheated very hot grill, or in a preheated oven. After charring, leave until cool enough to handle, then peel off the skin with a small, sharp knife.

PROSCIUTTO

Prosciutto crudo, usually labelled just 'prosciutto', is cured and salted raw ham. Made throughout Italy, various styles and qualities are available. Parma ham, which can only be made according to strict regulations around Parma, is generally considered the best, although some *aficionados* prefer San Daniele.

SAFFRON

Use pure saffron threads in preference to the powder which may have been adulterated. A mere pinch of saffron is all that is needed to flavour a dish for 4-6 people, so threads are not as expensive as they may first seem. Gently and lightly toasting the saffron threads in a dry, heavy frying pan

will bring out the flavour, and crushing them before adding to a dish will help them to dissolve more quickly.

SPICES

To walk around a spice souk is a heady and memorable experience. All around are large sacks brimming with mostly unidentifiable pods, seeds, buds, berries, roots and pieces of bark of varying hues, all exuding their own special fragrance, creating an exhilarating sensuous mélange. These spices are fresh and so have a stronger 'fresher' flavour than many sold here. It really is important not to store spices for long and to always keep them in a cool, dark place. I buy whole spices (except nutmeg) then grind them to order, after first dry-roasting them in a heavy frying pan for a minute or so.

SUN-DRIED TOMATOES

Choose plump, well-flavoured tomatoes, dried naturally under the hot Mediterranean sun. Cheap ones won't be genuine. Sun-dried tomatoes preserved in olive oil are more expensive than those in the dry form. The latter should be soaked in hot water for 1-1½ hours then dried with kitchen paper before using. To have a supply ready for use, soak several at a time then layer them in a jar with olive oil, seal and keep in a cool place. The oil from sun-dried tomatoes is ideal in salads and for brushing on crostinis and pizzas.

TOMATOES

The dire situation of flavourless, woolly tomatoes is being redressed, as most supermarkets now offer tomatoes 'grown for flavour'. Good tomatoes imported from Mediterranean countries are more easily available, too. To skin and seed tomatoes, pour boiling water over them, leave for 2-3 minutes, drain and slip off the skins when they are cool enough to handle. Cut in half and scoop out the seeds.

TAHINI

Also spelt 'tahina', this is a paste made from ground toasted sesame seeds. Brands differ in their flavour, so it may be worth trying a number to find one you like. Tahini separates if left to stand for a while and must be stirred thoroughly before using; I usually invert the jar for a while to make blending easier. Keep tahini in a cool place, but preferably not the refrigerator as this makes blending more difficult.

YOGURT

Greek strained ewes' milk yogurt is the type used in the southern and eastern Mediterranean and is now quite readily available here. It has a unique, mild creamy flavour with just a hint of acidity. Strained cows' milk yogurt falls short of this and ordinary cows' milk yogurt further still.

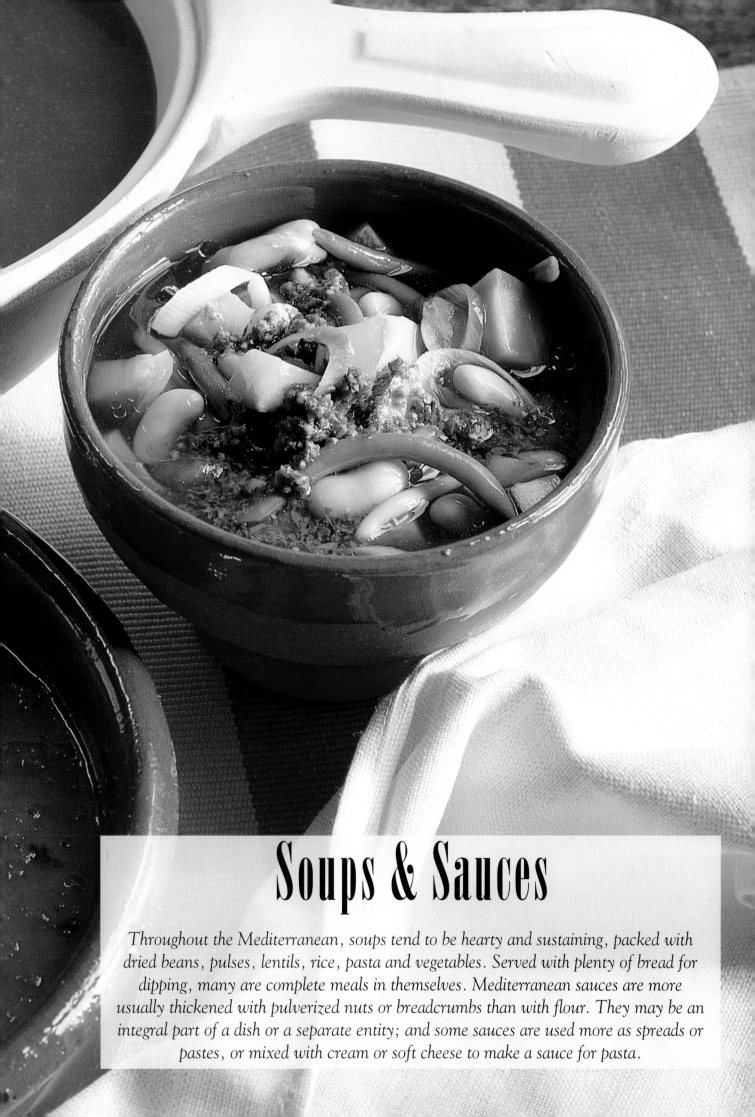

Soups & Sauces

Throughout the Mediterranean, soups tend to be hearty and sustaining, packed with dried beans, pulses, lentils, rice, pasta and vegetables. Served with plenty of bread for dipping, many are complete meals in themselves. Mediterranean sauces are more usually thickened with pulverized nuts or breadcrumbs than with flour. They may be an integral part of a dish or a separate entity; and some sauces are used more as spreads or pastes, or mixed with cream or soft cheese to make a sauce for pasta.

GAZPACHO

A bowl of chilled, colourful Gazpacho is one of the glories of Andalusian cooking and the epitome of hot weather food. Some sources claim that the soup dates back to before Roman times, others that it originated during the struggles against the Moorish invaders, but it could not have existed in the form we know it until after the sixteenth century when peppers and tomatoes were introduced to Spain. Gazpacho used to be served after the main course and before the fruit, but now its usual place is at the beginning of the meal. There are many recipes for Gazpacho, the varying proportions of ingredients resulting in endless changes of colour and taste. The success of any version, however, depends on the quality of the ingredients and on not allowing one flavour to dominate.

750 G (1½ LB) EXTRA LARGE TOMATOES, SKINNED, DESEEDED AND DICED

½ SPANISH ONION, CHOPPED

1 GREEN PEPPER, CORED, DESEEDED AND CHOPPED

1 RED PEPPER, CORED, DESEEDED AND CHOPPED

2 CLOVES OF GARLIC, CHOPPED

2 SLICES OF FIRM WHITE BREAD, CRUSTS REMOVED, BROKEN INTO PIECES

300 ML (½ PINT) TOMATO JUICE

3 TABLESPOONS VIRGIN OLIVE OIL

2 TABLESPOONS SHERRY VINEGAR

SALT AND PEPPER

ICE CUBES TO SERVE

ACCOMPANIMENTS

1 SMALL RED PEPPER, CORED, DESEEDED AND DICED

1 SMALL GREEN PEPPER, CORED, DESEEDED AND DICED

1 SMALL ONION, DICED

1 HARD-BOILED EGG, CHOPPED

CROUTONS (SEE NEXT RECIPE)

Put all the soup ingredients, except the ice cubes, in a food processor or blender. Mix until smooth, then pour through a nylon sieve, pressing down well on the contents of the sieve. If necessary, thin the soup with water, then chill well.

Place the accompaniments in separate bowls. Adjust the seasoning of the soup, if necessary, then pour into cold soup bowls. Add a few ice cubes to each bowl and serve with the accompaniments.

Serves 4

*Overleaf:
Clockwise from top: Gazpacho,
Grilled Mediterranean Vegetable Soup
and Soupe au Pistou*

GRILLED MEDITERRANEAN VEGETABLE SOUP

Featuring grilled aubergines, red peppers, tomatoes, garlic and herbs, this is for me the quintessential Mediterranean soup and one of my favourites, especially in summer. I do not bother to remove the seeds from the tomatoes, as they add interest to the soup's appearance.

1 LARGE ONION, HALVED BUT NOT PEELED

4 CLOVES OF GARLIC

4 RIPE BUT FIRM TOMATOES

2 AUBERGINES, TOTAL WEIGHT ABOUT 750 G (1½ LB), HALVED LENGTHWAYS

2 RED PEPPERS, HALVED

3 TABLESPOONS VIRGIN OLIVE OIL, PLUS EXTRA FOR BRUSHING

5 SPRIGS OF THYME

1 FRESH BAY LEAF, TORN

4-5 HALVES OF SUN-DRIED TOMATOES, CHOPPED

1.5 LITRES (2½ PINTS) GOOD CHICKEN OR VEGETABLE STOCK

6 LARGE BASIL LEAVES, TORN

LEMON JUICE TO TASTE

SALT AND PEPPER

TO SERVE

3 SLICES OF COUNTRY BREAD (SEE PAGE 113), CRUSTS REMOVED

OLIVE OIL

TORN BASIL LEAVES (OPTIONAL)

Cook the onion, garlic, ripe tomatoes, aubergines and peppers under a preheated hot grill until charred and softened. Cool slightly, then peel the onion, garlic and tomatoes. Remove the charred patches from the aubergines and red peppers and discard the pepper cores and seeds. Roughly chop them all.

Gently heat the olive oil with the thyme and bay leaf for a few minutes. Add the chopped vegetables, sun-dried tomatoes and stock, bring to the boil, cover and simmer gently for 20 minutes. Add the basil and simmer for a further 5 minutes. Cool slightly, then purée briefly in a blender or food processor at slow speed to retain some pieces of aubergine skin and pepper. Return to the pan, season and add lemon juice to taste. Reheat, but the soup is best if it is not too hot when eaten.

Just before serving, make the croûtons. Brush the bread with oil, cut into cubes and bake in a preheated oven, 200°C (400°F), Gas Mark 6, until crisp and golden. Serve the soup garnished with basil and accompanied by the croûtons.

Serves 4-6

SOUPE AU PISTOU

*This aromatic soup resembles a minestrone with pistou, a
type of pesto without pine nuts, added at the end.*

125 G (4 OZ) DRIED SOISSONS OR CANNELLINI BEANS, SOAKED

OVERNIGHT AND DRAINED

3 TABLESPOONS OLIVE OIL

2 LEEKS, WHITE PART ONLY, THINLY SLICED

2 CARROTS, CHOPPED

250 G (8 OZ) PUMPKIN, DESEEDED, PEELED AND COARSELY DICED

175 G (6 OZ) BROAD BEANS

175 G (6 OZ) FRENCH BEANS, CUT INTO 7-10 CM (3-4 INCH) LENGTHS

175 G (6 OZ) COURGETTES, CUT INTO CHUNKS

4 TOMATOES, SKINNED, DESEEDED AND CHOPPED

50 G (2 OZ) DRIED MACARONI OR SHELL PASTA

SALT AND PEPPER

PISTOU

25 G (I OZ) BASIL LEAVES

2 CLOVES OF GARLIC

50 G (2 OZ) PARMESAN CHEESE, FRESHLY GRATED

4-6 TABLESPOONS OLIVE OIL

SALT

TO SERVE

FRESHLY GRATED PARMESAN CHEESE

VIRGIN OLIVE OIL

Cook the dried beans in boiling water for 10 minutes, cover,
reduce the heat and simmer for 30 minutes. Drain, reserving
the water. Measure the water and make up to 1.5 litres
(2½ pints). Heat the oil in a saucepan, add the leeks and
cook, stirring occasionally, until softened. Stir in the carrots
and pumpkin and cook for 2-3 minutes before stirring in the
soissons or cannellini beans and reserved cooking liquid.
Cover and simmer gently for 45 minutes.

Add the remaining vegetables and pasta, season and cook
gently for a further 15 minutes until tender.

Meanwhile, make the pistou; tear the basil leaves and put
them in a mortar. Add the garlic and a pinch of salt and
pound to a paste using a pestle. Add half the cheese and
pound together. Mix with a little oil to moisten. Continue
adding cheese and oil until well and evenly mixed. Spoon the
pistou into a tureen, pour over the soup, cover and keep
warm for 5 minutes. Serve with more Parmesan and olive oil.

Serves 4-6

AVGOLEMONO SOUP

*The combination of eggs and lemon juice that is used as a
thickener, known as Avgolemono, is the favourite Greek
way of flavouring and thickening liquids at the same time.
The liquid may be a sauce to accompany a pilaf or stuffed
vine leaves, a casserole or, as here, a light fresh soup.
Containing few ingredients, the quality of the soup rests
mainly on the stock, which in coastal areas would be fish
stock, while inland it would be chicken or meat. A few
small pieces of fish, chicken or meat may be added and more
or less rice or eggs used, depending on the thickness and
type of soup required.*

1.2 LITRES (2 PINTS) GOOD FISH OR CHICKEN STOCK

50-75 G (2-3 OZ) LONG GRAIN RICE

3 TABLESPOONS FINELY CHOPPED PARSLEY

2 OR 3 EGGS, SIZE 2 OR 3

6 TABLESPOONS LEMON JUICE

SALT AND PEPPER

Bring the stock to the boil, add the rice, cover and simmer
for 15 minutes, or until the rice is tender. Add the parsley
and season to taste.

Beat the eggs with the lemon juice, then whisk in a little of
the hot stock. Very slowly pour the egg mixture into the
saucepan, stirring constantly over a very low heat; the soup
must not boil, otherwise it will curdle. Serve immediately.

Serves 4

TURKISH WALNUT SOUP

This inspired combination of walnuts and orange is based on a soup that I ate one day near Izmir. It was served in large, chunky bowls in a simple country restaurant, more like a private home than a commercial establishment. With the soup came a plate piled high with hunks of brown bread, warm from the oven, and a dish of pale, fresh unsalted butter – a veritable feast. In a quest to find the secret of its beauty, one of my companions enquired about the recipe, but his Turkish could not cope with the heavy dialect of the cook. However, I have subsequently discovered that plump, fresh nuts are essential for a good soup.

175 G (6 OZ) SHELLED WALNUTS

I TABLESPOON OLIVE OIL

4 SHALLOTS, CHOPPED

2 CLOVES OF GARLIC, CRUSHED

GOOD PINCH OF GROUND CINNAMON

GRATED RIND OF I ORANGE

JUICE OF 2 ORANGES

1.2 LITRES (2 PINTS) CHICKEN OR VEGETABLE STOCK

½ TABLESPOON WALNUT OIL

125 ML (4 FL OZ) GREEK STRAINED EWES' MILK YOGURT

SALT AND PEPPER

TO GARNISH

CHOPPED CORIANDER OR PARSLEY

GRATED ORANGE RIND

CHOPPED WALNUTS

Place the walnuts under a preheated grill until crisp, then coarsely chop them.

Meanwhile, heat the olive oil in a saucepan, add the shallots and cook, stirring occasionally, until softened but not coloured. Stir in the garlic, cook for 2 minutes and then stir in the cinnamon for about 30 seconds. Add the walnuts, orange rind and orange juice and boil for about I minute.

Tip the mixture into a blender or food processor, add a ladleful of the stock and the walnut oil and mix to a thick purée. Add a little more stock to thin the purée, then pour back into the saucepan, stir in the remaining stock, season and bring to the boil. Simmer for 5-10 minutes, stirring occasionally.

Over a low heat, whisk in the yogurt and heat through very gently; do not allow the soup to get too hot. Serve garnished with chopped coriander or parsley, grated orange rind and chopped walnuts.

Serves 4

PUMPKIN SOUP

Mantua is the home of quite a repertoire of renowned pumpkin dishes, including a most delicious risotto, delicate gnocchi and 'tortelli di zucca', which is traditionally served on Christmas Eve, as well as the best pumpkin soup I have ever encountered. In fact, pumpkin is eaten and enjoyed to such an extent in Mantua that it has become the town's emblem. What makes the Mantuan recipes so special is the particular type of pumpkin – the magnificent yellow-fleshed 'zucca gialla'. The nearest equivalent is butternut squash.

The soup is emulated elsewhere with many versions evolving. One that I highly recommend trying is flavoured with a smidgen of saffron, and it really does make an extremely good soup. In the recipe below, milk can be substituted for half the stock, but it should not be added until the soup is reheated after puréeing.

I KG (2 LB) BUTTERNUT SQUASH OR PUMPKIN

2 TABLESPOONS OLIVE OIL

125 G (4 OZ) PIECE OF PROSCIUTTO, CHOPPED

2 ONIONS, CHOPPED

600 ML (I PINT) CHICKEN OR VEGETABLE STOCK

I BAY LEAF

SPRIG OF THYME

SALT AND PEPPER

BASIL LEAVES TO GARNISH

CROUTONS TO SERVE (SEE GRILLED MEDITERRANEAN

VEGETABLE SOUP, PAGE 16)

Discard the seeds and stringy parts of the squash or pumpkin, cut the flesh from the skin and chop it.

Heat the oil in a large saucepan, add the prosciutto and onions and cook, stirring occasionally, until the onions are soft but not coloured. Stir in the squash or pumpkin for a few seconds, then add the stock, bay leaf and thyme. Bring to the boil, then simmer for 30 minutes until the squash or pumpkin is very tender.

Discard the herbs and purée the soup in a blender or food processor or pass it through a sieve. Return to the saucepan. Add the seasoning and reheat gently. Serve with basil leaves sprinkled over and accompanied by the croûtons.

Serves 4

Top: Turkish Walnut Soup
Bottom: Pumpkin Soup

FISH SOUP

To choose one specific type of fish soup or stew recipe was an impossible task, as a whole chapter could be devoted to authentic Mediterranean fish soups, let alone all the personal variations. Bouillabaisse had to be omitted because it needs fish only available from the Mediterranean. In the end I opted for a hybrid that includes the features I particularly like, such as a mixture of seafish and shellfish, whole pieces of fish, a garlicky aïoli thickening, and a crisp croûtes topping spread with 'hot' aïoli (definitely a main course soup), and have left others to make what adjustments they like. The most important principle is to use the freshest fish available and cook each type for its correct time.

1.75-2 KG (3½-4 LB) MIXED FISH WITH BONE, SUCH AS JOHN DORY,

GURNARD OR RED MULLET, SEA BREAM, MONKFISH, MUSSELS

AND UNCOOKED LARGE PRAWNS

EXTRA FISH HEADS AND BONES FOR THE STOCK

1 CARROT, HALVED

1 ONION, HALVED

BOUQUET GARNI OF 1 BAY LEAF, SEVERAL SPRIGS OF PARSLEY, 2 SPRIGS OF THYME

AND 3 SPRIGS OF FENNEL

175 ML (6 FL OZ) MEDIUM-BODIED DRY WHITE WINE

1.8 LITRES (3 PINTS) WATER

3 TABLESPOONS OLIVE OIL

2 LEEKS, THINLY SLICED

2 CLOVES OF GARLIC, CRUSHED

2 SUN-RIPENED EXTRA LARGE TOMATOES, SKINNED, DESEEDED AND CHOPPED

PINCH OF SAFFRON THREADS, TOASTED AND CRUSHED

½ RED PEPPER, CHARRED, CORED AND DESEEDED

DOUBLE QUANTITY AÏOLI (SEE PAGE 24)

PINCH OF CHILLI POWDER

4 EGG YOLKS

SALT AND PEPPER

TO SERVE

1 SMALL FRENCH STICK, SLICED AND DRIED IN A WARM OVEN UNTIL CRISP

FRESHLY GRATED PARMESAN CHEESE

Trim and clean the fish, reserving the heads and trimmings. Cut the fish into large chunks; remove the legs and any eggs from the prawns. Scrub and debeard the mussel shells.

Put all the fish bones, heads and trimmings into a large saucepan with the carrot, onion, bouquet garni, wine and water. Bring slowly to the boil, skim off the scum from the surface and simmer for 25 minutes. Strain through a muslin-lined sieve, pressing down well on the contents of the sieve.

Heat the oil in a large saucepan, add the leeks and garlic and cook, stirring occasionally, until softened but not coloured. Stir in the tomatoes and saffron and bring to the boil. Simmer for 2-3 minutes, then pour in the fish stock and return to the boil. Lower the heat and add the fish, except for the prawns and mussels. Poach for about 5 minutes before adding the mussels and prawns and cooking for a further 5 minutes – take care not to overcook the fish.

Meanwhile, crush the red pepper in a mortar or a bowl and mix in half the Aïoli with a pestle or the end of a rolling pin. Add chilli powder to taste. Spoon into a small serving bowl. Beat the egg yolks into the remaining Aïoli.

Using a slotted spoon, transfer the fish and shellfish to a large warm tureen; you can remove some or all of the skin and bones, if you like. Discard any mussels which have not opened. Cover and keep warm.

Stir a ladleful of the liquid into the Aïoli and egg yolk mixture. Lower the heat beneath the pan, then stir the Aïoli liquid into the pan. Heat gently, stirring constantly, until it begins to thicken; do not allow to boil. Adjust the seasoning to taste then pour over the fish. Spoon a few pieces of fish into each soup bowl, pour over a good ladle of soup, and serve with the French bread, red pepper sauce and Parmesan cheese so each person can spread sauce on the bread, place it on the soup and sprinkle over some Parmesan.

Serves 6

WHITE BEAN SOUP WITH GARLIC SAUCE

More or less identical soups based on dried white beans are popular in Italy, particularly Tuscany, as well as in Greece and Turkey.

6 TABLESPOONS OLIVE OIL

2 CLOVES OF GARLIC, CRUSHED

1 BAY LEAF

LEAVES FROM 2 SPRIGS OF THYME AND 2 SPRIGS OF OREGANO

1 SAGE LEAF, CHOPPED

375 G (12 OZ) CANNELLINI OR BORLOTTI BEANS, SOAKED OVERNIGHT AND DRAINED

1.8 LITRES (3 PINTS) BOILING WATER

1 LARGE ONION, CHOPPED

2 CARROTS, CHOPPED

1 HEAD OF CELERY, CHOPPED

SALT AND PEPPER

FINELY CHOPPED PARSLEY TO GARNISH

SAUCE

3 EGG YOLKS, SIZE 2

4 TABLESPOONS LEMON JUICE

3 CLOVES OF GARLIC, CRUSHED

175 G (6 OZ) UNSALTED BUTTER, MELTED UNTIL JUST BUBBLING

SALT AND PEPPER

Heat 4 tablespoons of the oil in a large heavy saucepan, add the garlic, herbs and beans and cook, stirring frequently, for about 5 minutes. Add the boiling water and simmer until the beans are tender, about 1 hour, depending on their age; add a little more water during cooking, if necessary.

Meanwhile, heat the remaining oil in an earthenware dish or frying pan, add the onion, carrots and celery, cover tightly and cook over a low heat, stirring occasionally, until soft, about 20 minutes.

Stir the vegetables into the beans and purée half the mixture in a blender or food processor. Return the purée to the remaining half, season and reheat gently.

To make the sauce, mix the egg yolks, lemon juice, garlic and seasoning in a blender. With the motor running, slowly add the melted butter and continue mixing for a few minutes to make a thick, creamy sauce. Transfer to a warm bowl.

To serve, pour the soup into individual bowls. Add a spoonful of the sauce to each and sprinkle with finely chopped parsley.

Serves 4

HARIRA

Spicy colourful Harira is a popular Moroccan dish.

250 G (8 OZ) LEAN LAMB, CUBED

2 TABLESPOONS OLIVE OIL

1 ONION, CHOPPED

125 G (4 OZ) CHICKPEAS, SOAKED OVERNIGHT AND DRAINED

1.5 LITRES (2½ PINTS) WATER

125 G (4 OZ) RED LENTILS

425 G (14 OZ) TOMATOES, SKINNED, DESEEDED AND CHOPPED

1 TABLESPOON TOMATO PUREE

1 TEASPOON GROUND CINNAMON

1 RED PEPPER, CORED, DESEEDED AND CHOPPED

50 G (2 OZ) LONG GRAIN RICE

BUNCH OF CORIANDER, CHOPPED

SALT AND PEPPER

Fry the lamb in the oil in a large saucepan until an even light brown. Stir in the onion and cook gently until softened. Add the chickpeas and water, bring to the boil, cover and simmer for 1 hour, or until the chickpeas are almost tender.

Add the lentils, tomatoes, tomato purée, cinnamon and red pepper and simmer for about 15 minutes. Add the rice, bring to the boil; simmer for further 15 minutes, until rice and lentils are tender. Stir in the coriander and seasoning.

Serves 6

ANCHOIDE

Serve Anchoïde as a dip for crudités, or spread on croûtes.

2 CLOVES OF GARLIC, CHOPPED

20 ANCHOVY FILLETS, RINSED IF NECESSARY

APPROXIMATELY 1½ TABLESPOONS TORN BASIL

5 TABLESPOONS VIRGIN OLIVE OIL

2-3 TEASPOONS RED WINE VINEGAR

2 TEASPOONS TOMATO PUREE, PREFERABLY SUN-DRIED (OPTIONAL)

PEPPER

Crush the garlic using a pestle and mortar, pound in the anchovies. Add the basil. Gradually pour in the oil in a slow trickle, pounding constantly, then the vinegar and purée, if using. Season. Keep in a covered glass jar in the refrigerator. Stir and adjust level of vinegar and basil before serving.

Serves 4

PESTO

Pesto is made all over Italy, but its 'home' is Liguria, where, in the mild climate, a special variety of small-leaved, richly flavoured basil thrives. The use of Pecorino Sardo, a Sardinian cheese, is a reminder that Genoa was part of the Sardinian kingdom until 1861. Using the traditional pestle and mortar produces Pesto with the best flavour and texture, but it is a little laborious. For many people, the speed and ease of using a blender outweighs the loss in quality, but for me this loss is too great and a mezzaluna produces a far more acceptable result. It is worth making a lot of Pesto when basil is in season. Either pack it into small, airtight pots and refrigerate (allow it to come to room temperature before using), or freeze it in ice cube trays and keep the cubes in a plastic bag ready for thawing individually in the refrigerator as required. When making Pesto purposely for freezing, I prefer not to add the cheese until it has thawed for use. The classic way of using Pesto is with trenette, the local Ligurian fettucine, but there are innumerable other uses for it – spooned on to sliced tomatoes, served with plainly cooked meats, poultry and fish, added to sauces, casseroles and soups, as a filling for rolled fish fillets, or mixed with soft cheese and slipped between the skin and flesh of chicken portions.

50 G (2 OZ) FRESH BASIL LEAVES

1-2 CLOVES OF GARLIC

2 TABLESPOONS PINE NUTS, LIGHTLY TOASTED

30 G (1¼ OZ) PARMESAN CHEESE, FRESHLY GRATED

1 TABLESPOON FRESHLY GRATED PECORINO SARDO CHEESE

APPROXIMATELY 100 ML (3½ FL OZ) VIRGIN OLIVE OIL

SALT AND PEPPER

Put the basil, garlic, pine nuts and a pinch of salt in a mortar and grind with a pestle until a paste forms. Alternatively, chop with a mezzaluna. Add the cheeses and mix in well.

Slowly pour in the oil, stirring vigorously with a wooden spoon. Add black pepper to taste, if liked.

Pesto can be kept in a tightly covered jar in the refrigerator for up to one week.
Serves 4

*Clockwise from bottom left: Pesto,
Aïoli, Tapenade, Skorthalia, Toulouse
Walnut Sauce, Anchoïde, Salmoriglio,
Salsa Verde; Centre: Sun-dried tomatoes*

TAPENADE

Tapenade comes from 'tapeno', the old Provençal word for caper, traditionally an important ingredient. Nowadays this is less so and capers are sometimes left out altogether.

200 G (7 OZ) NOYONS BLACK OLIVES, PITTED

50 G (2 OZ) CAPERS

4 ANCHOVY FILLETS, RINSED IF NECESSARY

1-2 CLOVES OF GARLIC, CRUSHED

1 TABLESPOON DIJON MUSTARD

125 ML (4 FL OZ) OLIVE OIL

1 TEASPOON CRUMBLED THYME

LEMON JUICE TO TASTE

PEPPER

Pound the olives, capers, anchovies, garlic and mustard together in a mortar to make a paste. Work in the oil a drop at a time, then add a little more quickly. Mix in the thyme, lemon juice and plenty of black pepper. Adjust the consistency (it should be a thick, spreadable paste) and pungency if necessary, adding more oil to mellow it. Tapenade can be kept in a tightly covered jar in the refrigerator for several weeks. Serve at room temperature.
Serves 4

SKORTHALIA

This pungent, Greek garlic sauce may be thickened with potato, bread or nuts, principally walnuts or almonds, and is served with poultry, fish (especially salt cod), grilled meats, vegetables, hard-boiled eggs and on bread.

4 SLICES OF BREAD, CRUSTS REMOVED, CRUMBLED

ABOUT 6 CLOVES OF GARLIC, CRUSHED

150 ML (¼ PINT) OLIVE OIL

3 TABLESPOONS LEMON JUICE

SALT AND PEPPER

Soak the bread in water, then squeeze it dry. Pound the garlic with a pinch of salt in a mortar with a pestle. Pound in the bread, then add the oil, a drop at a time at first, increasing the rate as the mixture begins to form a sauce, mixing all the time. Add lemon juice and pepper to taste.
Serves 4

SALMORIGLIO

Throughout Sicily, Salmoriglio is brushed on fish threaded on skewers before being grilled, then served separately with the fish. Sicilians believe the only way to make a really good Salmoriglio is to add seawater; in my kitchen, I've made the nearest replica I can by seasoning with sea salt.

1 TABLESPOON FINELY CHOPPED PARSLEY

1½ TEASPOONS CHOPPED OREGANO

APPROXIMATELY 1 TEASPOON FINELY CHOPPED ROSEMARY

1 CLOVE OF GARLIC, CRUSHED

175 ML (6 FL OZ) VIRGIN OLIVE OIL, WARMED SLIGHTLY

3 TABLESPOONS HOT WATER

ABOUT 4 TABLESPOONS LEMON JUICE

SEA SALT AND PEPPER

Pound together herbs, garlic and a pinch of salt in a mortar and pestle. Pour oil into a warmed bowl, then, using a fork, gradually whisk in the hot water then the lemon juice to make a thick, creamy sauce. Add herb mixture and pepper to taste, then place bowl over a saucepan of hot water for 5 minutes, whisking frequently. Serve in a warm sauceboat.
Serves 6

SALSA VERDE

This sauce is traditionally served with 'bollito misto', a north Italian dish of mixed boiled meats and poultry.

2 SLICES OF BREAD, CRUSTS REMOVED, SOAKED IN WHITE WINE VINEGAR

1 HARD-BOILED EGG, CHOPPED

3 ANCHOVY FILLETS, RINSED IF NECESSARY

LEAVES FROM A GOOD HANDFUL OF PARSLEY

1 DRIED RED CHILLI, CRUSHED

1 TABLESPOON BALSAMIC VINEGAR

1 TABLESPOON WHITE WINE VINEGAR

APPROXIMATELY 325 ML (11 FL OZ) OLIVE OIL

2 CLOVES OF GARLIC, HALVED LENGTHWAYS

Squeeze the bread dry and pass through a sieve, with the egg and the anchovies, into a mortar. Pound in the parsley and chilli, mix in the vinegars. Gradually beat in the oil using a fork or wire whisk. Add the garlic, cover and leave in the refrigerator for 1 day. Remove the garlic before serving.
Serves 6-8

AÏOLI AND AL-I-OLI

Aïoli is a Provençal sauce, which nowadays has come to be no more than mayonnaise with a garlic purée base, although originally it was based on breadcrumbs. True Catalan Al-i-oli, however, should be made from just garlic ('al') and ('i') oil ('oli'), so it is white and shiny with a pronounced garlic flavour. Without eggs, it is trickier to make than Aïoli because the emulsion does not form readily and is less stable. Use a mild, sweet, clean-tasting olive oil and plump, crisp garlic that is as fresh as possible. As when making mayonnaise, all the ingredients must be at room temperature. Both sauces should be thicker than mayonnaise and, traditionally, are quite dense. Using a food processor or blender will alter this characteristic, as they incorporate air, thus changing their qualities. Aïoli and Al-i-oli have innumerable uses – served with grilled poultry, fish, meats and rabbit, with vegetables and eggs and spread on bread. Aïoli can also be used to thicken and flavour many recipes, such as seafood, noodle and rice dishes, soups and casseroles.

Aïoli

6-12 CLOVES OF GARLIC, CHOPPED

2 EGG YOLKS

½-1 TEASPOON DIJON MUSTARD (OPTIONAL)

APPROXIMATELY 300 ML (½ PINT) OLIVE OIL

1½-2 TABLESPOONS LEMON JUICE, WHITE WINE VINEGAR OR

A COMBINATION OF THE TWO

SALT AND PEPPER

Crush the garlic with a pinch of salt in a mortar using a pestle until mixed to a smooth paste, then work in the egg yolks, and mustard if using. Add the oil, a few drops at a time, while stirring slowly, evenly and constantly in the same direction. Once half the oil has been incorporated, add half the lemon juice, white wine vinegar or combination, adding the remainder when all the oil has been incorporated.

Al-i-oli – omit the egg yolks, mustard and pepper, and – according to some sources – the lemon juice or vinegar. Reduce the quantity of oil to about 250 ml (8 fl oz) and stop adding it when an emulsion forms – to continue will cause the emulsion to 'break'. Serve immediately.

Al-i-oli and Aïoli with Roasted Garlic – use more cloves of roasted garlic for a sweeter, milder flavour.
Serves 4

NUT SAUCES

There are a number of different sauces based on ground nuts. In the Middle East and Turkey, all nut sauces tend to go under the name of tarator, although they may taste quite different. Traditionally, nut sauces are made using a pestle and mortar, but you could add the whole nuts to a small blender, and add the soaked bread and garlic. Mix together and slowly pour in the oil, mixing at slow speed and increasing the flow as the sauce thickens. Add lemon juice, water and seasoning as required. Serve at room temperature or lightly chilled, with fish, chicken, meats and vegetables.

LEBANESE TARATOR WITH PINE NUTS

1½ SLICES OF COUNTRY BREAD (SEE PAGE 113), CRUSTS REMOVED, TORN

1-2 CLOVES OF GARLIC, CRUSHED

250 G (8 OZ) PINE NUTS, CHOPPED

200-250 ML (7-8 FL OZ) OLIVE OIL

2-3 TABLESPOONS LEMON JUICE

SALT AND WHITE PEPPER

Soak the bread in a little water. Pound the garlic with a little salt in a mortar, then add and pound the nuts. Squeeze the bread dry, then work it into the sauce. Gradually mix in the oil, followed by lemon juice to taste and enough of the water to give a smooth light cream. Season to taste.
Serves 4

TURKISH TARATOR WITH HAZELNUTS, OR WALNUTS

1 SLICE OF COUNTRY BREAD (SEE PAGE 113), CRUSTS REMOVED

1 PLUMP CLOVE OF GARLIC, CRUSHED

125 G (4 OZ) HAZELNUTS OR WALNUTS, AS FRESH AS POSSIBLE, CHOPPED

125-150 ML (4-5 FL OZ) CHICKEN STOCK

APPROXIMATELY 2 TABLESPOONS LEMON JUICE

SALT AND PEPPER

Soak the bread in a little water. Pound the garlic with a little salt in a mortar. Add and pound the hazelnuts or walnuts. Squeeze the bread dry and work it into the sauce, followed by the chicken stock, lemon juice and pepper to taste.
Serves 4

TARATOR WITH TAHINI

2 CLOVES OF GARLIC

125 G (4 OZ) TAHINI

50-125 ML (2-4 FL OZ) WATER

APPROXIMATELY 125 ML (4 FL OZ) LEMON JUICE

SALT AND PEPPER

Crush the garlic with pinch of salt, then beat in the tahini using a wooden spoon. Alternately beat in a little water and lemon juice; the former thickens the sauce, the latter thins it. Incorporate all of the lemon juice and sufficient water to give a sauce of the desired consistency, depending on its use. Season with salt and pepper.
Serves 4

Variation

Tarator with Tahini and Parsley – add a handful of finely chopped parsley after all the lemon juice and about half of the water have been added. Do not add more water unless the mixture is too thick. Serve as a dip or an accompaniment to simple fish dishes.

TOULOUSE WALNUT SAUCE (AILLADE)

125 G (4 OZ) WALNUTS, AS FRESH AS POSSIBLE

2 CLOVES OF GARLIC, CRUSHED

75 ML (3 FL OZ) LIGHT OLIVE OIL

75 ML (3 FL OZ) WALNUT OIL

LEMON JUICE

2 TABLESPOONS WATER

CHOPPED PARSLEY OR CHIVES

SALT AND PEPPER

Lightly toast the walnuts, leave to cool slightly then chop roughly. Pound the garlic with a little salt in a mortar, then add and pound the walnuts. Gradually mix in the oils, followed by lemon juice to taste and enough of the water to give a smooth light cream. Season to taste. Just before serving, sprinkle with parsley or chives.
Serves 6

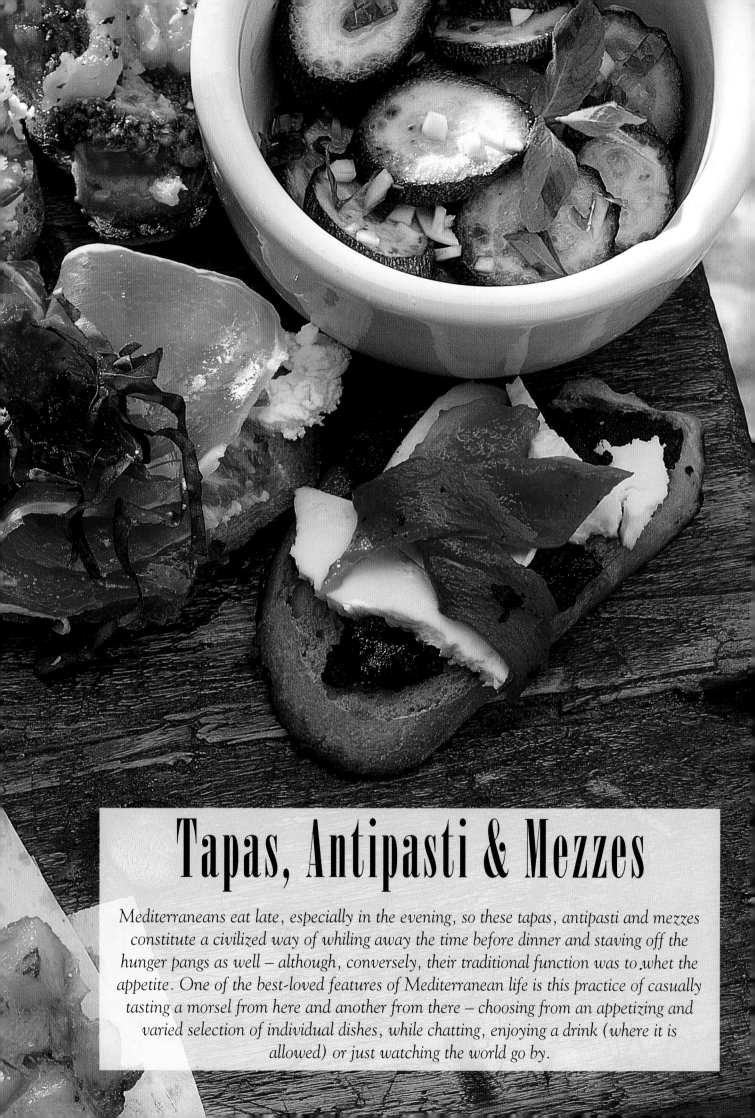

Tapas, Antipasti & Mezzes

Mediterraneans eat late, especially in the evening, so these tapas, antipasti and mezzes constitute a civilized way of whiling away the time before dinner and staving off the hunger pangs as well – although, conversely, their traditional function was to whet the appetite. One of the best-loved features of Mediterranean life is this practice of casually tasting a morsel from here and another from there – choosing from an appetizing and varied selection of individual dishes, while chatting, enjoying a drink (where it is allowed) or just watching the world go by.

MARINATED COURGETTES

Marinating foods, 'a scapece', is a very old method of preservation. Some say the name is derived from that of Apicius, the author of the earliest known cookery book, De Re Coquinaria. Nowadays, the method is used simply as another way of preparing foods, usually fish and vegetables. Here, the combination of courgettes, lemon and herbs makes a light and refreshing dish.

750 G (1½ LB) COURGETTES, CUT INTO 5 MM (¼ INCH) SLICES

OLIVE OIL

LEAVES FROM A BUNCH OF BASIL

3 TABLESPOONS MINT LEAVES

2 SMALL CLOVES OF GARLIC, FINELY CHOPPED

2 TABLESPOONS LEMON JUICE

SALT AND PEPPER

Layer the courgette slices and salt in a colander and leave for 30 minutes. Rinse the courgettes well and pat dry.

Heat a 5 mm (1/4 inch) layer of oil in a large frying pan, add the courgette slices in batches so they are not crowded and cook for about 3 minutes each side until golden. Using a slotted spoon, transfer to kitchen paper to drain.

Arrange the slices on a plate, tucking basil and mint leaves between them. Sprinkle with the garlic, lemon juice and seasonings and leave for at least 2 hours, preferably overnight, in the refrigerator, but return to room temperature about 30 minutes before serving.
Serves 4

BROAD BEANS WITH HAM

I have sampled innumerable variations on the theme of broad beans and ham. Some have been more or less just the beans and ham; at Rondena, in Andalusia, the cooking juices were thickened with breadcrumbs and chopped hard-boiled egg was added, whereas in the colder climate of the Asturias, carrots and potatoes padded out the dish. However, this particularly colourful and tasty version is my favourite.

2 TABLESPOONS OLIVE OIL

4 LARGE SPRING ONIONS, FINELY CHOPPED

I RED PEPPER, CORED, DESEEDED AND DICED

50 G (2 OZ) SERRANO HAM, DICED

500 G (I LB) SHELLED BROAD BEANS

APPROXIMATELY 175 ML (6 FL OZ) MEDIUM-BODIED DRY

WHITE WINE

SALT AND PEPPER

Heat the oil in a saucepan and add the spring onions, red pepper and ham and cook for 3 minutes. Stir in the beans for I minute, then add sufficient wine to cover the vegetables. Bring quickly to the boil, cover the pan and simmer gently until the beans are tender, about 15-20 minutes. Uncover and boil off excess liquid, if necessary. Add pepper and salt if necessary – this will depend on the saltiness of the ham. Cool slightly before serving.
Serves 4

Variation

Greek Broad Beans with Dill – gently cook 2 bunches of sliced, plump spring onions in 3 tablespoons olive oil in a heavy pan, until soft. Stir in 625 g (1¼ lb) shelled fresh young broad beans and cook gently for 2-3 minutes. Add 2-3 tablespoons chopped dill, salt and pepper and sufficient water to just cover the beans. Cover and cook gently until the beans are tender. Serve with Greek ewes' milk yogurt.

Overleaf:
Clockwise from top right: Marinated Courgettes, Crostini, Tortilla with Red Pepper, Marinated Olives and Broad Beans with Ham

MARINATED OLIVES

With about 190 million olive trees in Spain it is no surprise that olives appear at virtually every tapas bar and almost automatically accompany every alcoholic drink. Marinating olives with herbs and spices gives additional distinction and is a way for a bar to personalize the olives it serves.

500 G (1 LB) GREEN OR BLACK OLIVES

1 FRESH RED CHILLI, DESEEDED AND CHOPPED

4 CLOVES OF GARLIC, CRUSHED

1 SPRIG OF OREGANO

1 SPRIG OF THYME

1 TEASPOON FINELY CHOPPED ROSEMARY

2 BAY LEAVES

1 TEASPOON FENNEL SEEDS, BRUISED

1 TEASPOON ROASTED AND FINELY CRUSHED CUMIN SEEDS

OLIVE OIL TO COVER

Using a small sharp knife make a lengthways slit through to the stone of each olive. Put the olives into a bowl and stir in the chilli, garlic, oregano, thyme, rosemary, bay leaves, fennel seeds and cumin.

Pack the olive mixture into a screw-top jar and cover with olive oil. Close the jar and leave the olives for at least 3 days, shaking jar occasionally, before using. If stored in a cool, dark place the olives will keep for several months.
Serves 4

CROSTINI

Crostini are simply slices of bread toasted in the oven, topped with something savoury and served warm. They may be first rubbed with garlic then trickled with good olive oil. The bread is very important – the edges should be firm and crusty, while the middle should have a chewy texture that is able to absorb any juices that might seep from the topping. Good examples are Italian and French country bread and ciabatta.

Cut the bread into 1 cm (½ inch) thick slices then bake in a single layer on a baking tray in a preheated oven, 200°C (400°F), Gas Mark 6, until lightly browned, turning once, for 5-10 minutes.
Serves 4

CROSTINI TOPPINGS

• tapenade, anchoïde, pesto, perhaps topped with a slice of tomato.
• tapenade, anchoïde, pesto, topped with a slice of mozzarella cheese and chopped or sliced tomato; pop back into the oven for a few minutes.
• soft goats' cheese mixed with chopped basil or tarragon or thyme, topped with sliced sun-dried tomatoes.
• sun-dried tomato purée sprinkled with Pecorino and grilled.
• cold, thick peperonata, ratatouille, caponata.
• grated Scamorza cheese (smoked mozzarella), sprinkled with a little finely chopped sage, seasoned and trickled with olive oil; grill until the cheese melts.
• sliced mozzarella cheese topped with a slice of aubergine, sprinkled with grated mozzarella and chopped parsley and basil; then grilled until the cheese has melted and turned golden.
• Gorgonzola mashed with a little cream, topped with chopped walnuts; then popped under a hot grill.
• warm asparagus spears sprinkled with lemon juice on anchoïde, placed briefly under the grill. Finish with finely chopped hard-boiled egg, if liked.
• chicken livers or wild, shiitake or oyster mushrooms sautéed in olive oil with finely chopped red onion and garlic; mash with a little chopped sage and seasoning.
• spread with 125 g (4 oz) pitted black, oil-packed olives coarsely puréed with 125 ml (4 fl oz) olive oil, 125 g (4 oz) oil-packed sun-dried tomatoes, 2 teaspoons Dijon mustard, 2 teaspoons lemon juice and pepper; garnish with basil or parsley.
• 750 g (1½ lb) sun-ripened tomatoes, skinned, deseeded and chopped, mixed with the chopped leaves of a bunch of basil, 4 finely chopped cloves of garlic and 4 tablespoons virgin olive oil. Leave for 30 minutes, then stir in 150 g (5 oz) black oil-packed olives, pitted and chopped. Add pepper to taste. Garnish with strips of anchovy fillet and basil sprigs.

SPINACH-STUFFED MUSHROOMS

On most mornings when we were staying in a 'mas', a stone farmhouse, nestled secretively in the hills behind Aix-en-Provence, we would be at the daily markets in the town soon after they opened at 8.00 am, so that we could take our pick of the choicest finds – fist-sized Cavaillon melons, dried lime blossom ('tilleul'), for delicate tea and poached chicken, sweet peaches and nectarines, black figs with their scarlet interiors, large courgette blossoms, small peppers and aubergines and whatever wild mushrooms resulted from early morning walks through the countryside. Back at the farmhouse we often turned the vegetables and courgette flowers into a selection of Provençal petits farcis. This is the recipe we used for the mushrooms.

275 G (9 OZ) SPINACH, STALKS REMOVED

400 G (13 OZ) MEDIUM CAP MUSHROOMS

2 TABLESPOONS OLIVE OIL, PLUS EXTRA FOR BRUSHING

25 G (1 OZ) BACON, CHOPPED

1 SMALL SHALLOT, FINELY CHOPPED

1 CLOVE OF GARLIC, FINELY CHOPPED

65 G (2½ OZ) SOFT GOATS' CHEESE

APPROXIMATELY 25 G (1 OZ) PARMESAN CHEESE,

FRESHLY GRATED

2 TABLESPOONS FRESH BREADCRUMBS

SALT AND PEPPER

Wash the spinach but do not dry it. Put it into a saucepan and cook, stirring occasionally, until wilted and no liquid is visible. Tip into a colander and squeeze out as much liquid as possible. Chop finely. Snap the stalks from the mushrooms and chop them finely.

Heat the oil in a frying pan, add the bacon, shallot, garlic and mushroom stalks and cook, stirring occasionally, for about 5 minutes. Stir in the spinach. Soon afterwards, remove the pan from the heat and stir in the goats' cheese, and salt and pepper.

Brush the mushroom caps with oil and place them, gills uppermost, in a single layer in an oiled shallow baking dish. Divide the spinach mixture between the mushrooms. Mix together the Parmesan cheese and breadcrumbs, sprinkle over the mushrooms and bake in a preheated oven, 190°C (375°F), Gas Mark 5, for about 20 minutes, until the mushrooms are tender. Serve warm.

Serves 4

MUSHROOMS WITH GARLIC AND PARSLEY

To be truly authentic wild mushrooms should be used, the exact type changing with the time of year, but I think oyster mushrooms are perfectly acceptable to use, or failing those, brown cap (chestnut), mushrooms. The recipe is more usually made without the pine nuts, but I like the contrasting texture and flavour they bring.

3 TABLESPOONS OLIVE OIL

2 CLOVES OF GARLIC, FINELY CHOPPED

500 G (1 LB) OYSTER MUSHROOMS, CUT INTO LARGE PIECES

4 TABLESPOONS FINO SHERRY

50 G (2 OZ) PINE NUTS

SQUEEZE OF LEMON JUICE

2 TABLESPOONS CHOPPED PARSLEY

SALT AND PEPPER

Heat the oil in a large frying pan and add the garlic. Cook over a fairly high heat until it is just beginning to brown, about 3 minutes.

Stir in the mushrooms, sherry and pine nuts and continue to cook until the mushroom juices have almost evaporated. Add lemon juice and salt and pepper to taste, stir in the parsley and serve.

Serves 4

Left: Spinach-stuffed Mushrooms
Right: Mushrooms with Garlic and Parsley

TORTILLA WITH RED PEPPER

The 'classic' tortilla contains only potatoes and, perhaps, onion, but I prefer to add some other flavourings as well, such as red pepper and chorizo. Another favourite that I make when fleshy artichokes are around is tortilla with artichoke and serrano ham.

6 TABLESPOONS OLIVE OIL

425 G (14 OZ) POTATOES, DICED

1 SPANISH ONION, CHOPPED

1 LARGE RED PEPPER, CORED, DESEEDED AND CHOPPED

5 EGGS

150 G (5 OZ) CHORIZO, CHOPPED

SALT AND PEPPER

Heat the oil in a large, heavy frying pan, preferably non-stick. Season the potatoes and onion and add to the pan with the red pepper. Cook, covered, over a low heat until soft but not brown, about 20 minutes, stirring gently occasionally to prevent sticking. Drain off and reserve the oil.

In a small bowl, lightly beat the eggs with a little seasoning. Mix in the potatoes, onions, red pepper and chorizo and leave for 10 minutes.

Wipe the pan with kitchen paper and add enough of the reserved oil to cover the base with a thin film. Add the egg mixture, spreading it evenly in the pan. Cook over a moderate heat, shaking the pan occasionally, until the underside is set and beginning to brown.

Cover the pan with a large plate and hold it in place with one hand. Quickly invert the pan so the omelette falls on to the plate. Return the pan to the heat, add a little more oil and slide the omelette back into the pan, with the cooked side uppermost. Continue to cook until lightly browned underneath. Slide on to a serving plate and serve warm or at room temperature.

Serves 4 as a main course, or 8 for tapa

BLACK FIGS WITH MASCARPONE AND PROSCIUTTO

This recipe takes the well-known and equally well-loved combination of figs and Parma ham one stage further.

3 PLUMP, RIPE BLACK FIGS, QUARTERED

150 ML (¼ PINT) RICH FRENCH DRESSING

12 THIN SLICES OF PARMA HAM

12 HEAPED TEASPOONS MASCARPONE CHEESE

MINT LEAVES TO GARNISH

Toss the figs in the French dressing. Lay out the slices of ham and fold the long sides in to the middle. Place a fig quarter and a teaspoon of cheese at the end of each slice, then roll up to enclose. Place seam-side down on a serving plate. Garnish with mint leaves.

Serves 4

SCALLOPS WITH DILL

12 SCALLOPS, SHELLED

½ CUCUMBER, PEELED AND HALVED LENGTHWAYS

8 TABLESPOONS LEMON JUICE

2 TABLESPOONS CHOPPED DILL

1 TABLESPOON CHOPPED MINT

1 TABLESPOON VIRGIN OLIVE OIL

SALT AND PEPPER

LEMON SLICES AND MINT LEAVES TO GARNISH

If necessary, remove and discard from the scallop bodies the white muscle opposite the corals. Separate the corals from the bodies, then slice the bodies in half horizontally. Season with pepper.

Scoop out and discard the seeds from the cucumber and cut the flesh into pieces about the same size as the scallops. Add to boiling salted water, boil for 1 minute and drain.

Thread scallops, cucumber and corals on skewers alternately, then lay in a shallow non-metallic dish. Mix together the lemon juice, herbs and oil, pour over the scallops and cucumber, turn to coat with the marinade and leave for about 1 hour. Transfer the skewers to a grill rack and place under a preheated hot grill for 8-10 minutes, brushing with the remaining marinade occasionally and turning halfway through. Serve garnished with lemon slices and mint leaves.

Serves 4 as a first course, 2 as a light main course

PICKLED TURNIPS

Pickled turnips are very popular in the Middle East. Large jars of them are prepared by many families and they are a common sight in shop and restaurant windows, for sale in the streets and at the table. Even so, I had not expected them to be particularly to my taste, and I was very pleasantly surprised when I took my first bite of the pretty pink vegetable – it had a delicate, sweet sharpness and light crispness that I instantly found most appealing.

50 G (2 OZ) COARSE SALT

500 ML (17 FL OZ) WATER

250 ML (8 FL OZ) WHITE WINE VINEGAR

1 KG (2 LB) SMALL TURNIPS, HALVED

1 SMALL UNCOOKED BEETROOT, PEELED AND SLICED

2-4 CLOVES OF GARLIC (OPTIONAL)

FEW CELERY LEAVES

Bring the salt and water to the boil over a low heat, stirring. Remove from the heat, add the vinegar and leave to cool.

Layer the turnips, beetroot slices, garlic, if used, and the celery leaves in a sterilized preserving jar. Pour the cooled brine over the vegetables to cover them completely. Slip a fine knife or skewer down the inside of the jar in several places to dislodge any air bubbles. Place a small saucer, or something similar that will fit inside the jar, on top of the turnips, with a weight on top if necessary. Close the jar tightly and leave on a sunny window sill, or any other warm place for about 2 weeks.

The pickled turnips will keep for 2-3 months in the refrigerator.

Serves 4

GRILLED RADICCHIO

The most famous and best radicchio comes from Treviso, near Venice. It is a winter vegetable, cultivated under straw and as the heads grow through the straw, they look like red snowdrops. With spear-shaped, crisp leaves, radicchio di Treviso looks something like a small, red Cos lettuce and has a unique flavour. Unfortunately, it is hard, but not impossible, to find here; instead we usually have a variety recently developed by growers near Chioggia, south of Venice. It grows all year round, looks more like a round cabbage and tastes slightly more bitter. Nevertheless, I have never had any complaints when I have served these grilled heads with the savoury, melting surprise that oozes from the centre.

4 SMALL HEADS OF RADICCHIO

4 X 25 G (1 OZ) MINIATURE MOZZARELLA BALLS

(*BOCCONCINI*), DRAINED

4 SMALL ANCHOVY FILLETS, COARSELY CHOPPED

2 TEASPOONS FINELY CHOPPED PARSLEY

CRUSHED DRIED RED CHILLI (OPTIONAL)

EXTRA VIRGIN OLIVE OIL

PEPPER

LEMON WEDGES TO SERVE

Gently open out the leaves of each head of radicchio and place a ball of mozzarella in the centre; remove 1 or 2 of the inner leaves if necessary. Top with one quarter of the anchovy and parsley. Season with black pepper, and crushed chilli, if liked, and trickle over a few drops of olive oil. Carefully close the leaves over the cheese and secure with wooden cocktail sticks.

Brush the radicchio with olive oil then cook under a preheated moderate grill, turning occasionally, for about 8 minutes, until golden. Remove the cocktail sticks and serve immediately with lemon wedges.

Serves 4

Variation

Grilled Radicchio with Goats' Cheese – halve 2 small heads of radicchio lengthways and remove a few of the central leaves to form a hollow. Place, cut side up in a grill pan. Place a slice of goats' cheese in each hollow, brush the leaves and cheese with olive oil then grill until the cheese is bubbling. Sprinkle with chopped thyme or torn basil.

GNOCCHI

Gnocchi can be made from potatoes and flour, from pumpkin, a mixture of spinach and ricotta cheese, or from semolina (which, in reality are baked discs of polenta made with milk instead of water). The essence of all good gnocchi, no matter from what they are made, is their lightness. Gnocchi are usually simmered in water, then served simply with melted butter and grated Parmesan cheese or a sauce such as Gorgonzola or tomato. The ridges on gnocchi are not purely cosmetic; they make the cooking quicker and more even throughout and provide a surface for the sauce to cling to. Potato gnocchi are the most common type. The quantity of flour and egg will depend on the type and dryness of the potatoes.

625 G (1¼ LB) FLOURY POTATOES, SUCH AS KING EDWARD

1 EGG, BEATEN

PINCH OF GRATED NUTMEG (OPTIONAL)

APPROXIMATELY 200 G (7 OZ) PLAIN FLOUR

SALT AND PEPPER

GORGONZOLA SAUCE OR PESTO (SEE PAGE 23) TO SERVE

Boil the potatoes in their skins until tender. Drain and, protecting your hand with a tea towel, peel the hot potatoes, then pass through a vegetable mill or sieve. Mix in the egg, nutmeg, if liked, seasonings, and about half of the flour. Gradually add more flour until the mixture is soft, smooth and slightly sticky. Shape into rolls about 2.5 cm (1 inch) in diameter, then cut into 2 cm (¾ inch) pieces.

To shape the gnocchi, hold a fork in one hand, take 1 piece of gnocchi in the other and press it lightly with the thumb of your other hand against the inner curve of the prongs. Then, with a quick downwards movement, flip it towards the ends of the prongs so the gnocchi is concave on the thumb side, convex and ridged on the other. Gently lower the gnocchi in batches into plenty of just simmering salted water and poach until they come to the surface. Leave for a few seconds, then transfer to a warmed serving dish and serve with Gorgonzola sauce or Pesto.
Serves 6-8

Variation
Spinach and Potato Gnocchi – mix 75 g (3 oz) cooked and thoroughly drained spinach into the potatoes after sieving them.

SPINACH AND RICOTTA GNOCCHI

The lightest, most tender and delicious gnocchi, these are my favourite. However, if due diligence is not paid to drying the spinach adequately, the gnocchi are liable to disintegrate when cooked. So be warned. Without flour, the gnocchi are very delicate and need careful handling, so you may prefer to incorporate a couple of spoonfuls.

1 KG (2 LB) FRESH SPINACH

APPROXIMATELY 2 TABLESPOONS PLAIN FLOUR (OPTIONAL)

1 EGG, SIZE 1, BEATEN

250 G (8 OZ) FRESH RICOTTA CHEESE

50 G (2 OZ) PARMESAN CHEESE, FRESHLY GRATED

PINCH OF FRESHLY GRATED NUTMEG

SEASONED PLAIN FLOUR FOR COATING

SALT AND PEPPER

TO SERVE

MELTED UNSALTED BUTTER

FRESHLY GRATED PARMESAN CHEESE

Remove the stalks from the spinach, then wash but do not dry the leaves. Chop them and heat in a saucepan until they wilt and any visible liquid has disappeared. Tip into a sieve and squeeze out as much liquid as possible – this is very important. Return to the saucepan, add the flour, if using, and heat gently, stirring to complete the drying. Remove from the heat, beat in the egg and mix in the two cheeses, nutmeg and seasoning.

Break off small balls of the mixture and roll lightly in seasoned flour to coat lightly and evenly and form into gnocchi (see recipe left). Continue with the remaining mixture, then chill for about 1 hour.

Half fill a large frying pan with water, bring to simmering point then carefully lower in some of the spinach shapes, but do not crowd the pan. Poach until they rise to the surface. Using a slotted spoon, transfer to a warm plate. Cook the remaining shapes in the same way. Serve warm with melted butter trickled over and sprinkled with Parmesan cheese.
Serves 4

Left: Spinach and Ricotta Gnocchi
Right: Gnocchi

HUMMUS

I have been imprecise about quantities for this chickpea and sesame dip because people's tastes vary considerably, but the flavour of sesame should not overtake that of the chickpeas. Egyptians flavour the purée with enough cumin so that it is apparent but not dominant. The traditional garnish is pomegranate seeds. Whole cooked chickpeas are sometimes used instead, and ground cumin or chopped parsley sprinkled over the top with the paprika.

250 G (8 OZ) CHICKPEAS, SOAKED OVERNIGHT AND DRAINED

2-3 CLOVES OF GARLIC, CRUSHED

APPROXIMATELY 250 ML (8 FL OZ) LEMON JUICE

APPROXIMATELY 5 TABLESPOONS TAHINI

SALT

WARM PITTA BREAD TO SERVE

TO GARNISH

OLIVE OIL

PAPRIKA

Cook the chickpeas in plenty of boiling water until soft – 1-1½ hours depending on their quality and age. Drain and reserve the cooking liquid. Purée the chickpeas in a blender or food processor with a little of the cooking liquid, then press the purée through a sieve to remove the skins.

Crush the garlic with a little salt and beat into the chickpea purée. Stir in the lemon juice and tahini alternately, tasting before it has all been added to get the right balance of flavours. Add a little more salt, if necessary, and more of the cooking liquid to make a soft, creamy consistency. Spoon the purée into a shallow dish, cover and leave in the refrigerator for several hours.

Return to room temperature a short while before serving so that the purée is not too cold. Create swirls in the surface with the back of a spoon then trickle olive oil into the whirls and sprinkle lightly with paprika. Serve with warm pitta bread.

Serves 6

AUBERGINE DIP

I have eaten many mezzes but, without doubt, the best were the 25 that the ever-helpful team at the Dubai Hilton rustled up at a moment's notice for me to try. Their way with the aubergine dip, which I always follow now, was to leave some texture to it, rather than reducing the flesh to an homogenous purée, and not to dilute it with tahini or yogurt, as is sometimes the case.

APPROXIMATELY 1.1 KG (2¼ LB) AUBERGINES

APPROXIMATELY 4 TABLESPOONS FAIRLY MILD OLIVE OIL

APPROXIMATELY 3 TABLESPOONS LEMON JUICE

2 CLOVES OF GARLIC, VERY FINELY CHOPPED

40 G (1½ OZ) MILD ONION, VERY FINELY CHOPPED

1½ TABLESPOONS VERY FINELY CHOPPED RED PEPPER

SALT AND PEPPER

WARM PITTA BREAD TO SERVE

TO GARNISH

OLIVE OIL

CHOPPED PARSLEY

Grill the aubergines, turning frequently, until the skin is charred and blistered and the flesh feels soft when the aubergine is pressed. When cool enough to handle, remove and discard the stems and skin. Squeeze the flesh gently to expel surplus liquid.

Chop the aubergine flesh so that it still has some texture. Place in a bowl and pour in the oil. Mix in most of the lemon juice and stir in the garlic, onion, red pepper and salt and pepper. Taste and add more lemon juice, if necessary. Cover and leave in the refrigerator for several hours.

Return to room temperature a short while before serving so that the purée is not too cold. Spoon it into a flat dish and make a few swirls in the surface with the back of a spoon. Pour a thin trickle of olive oil into the whirls and garnish with chopped parsley. Serve with warm pitta bread.

Serves 6

TABBOULEH

I have been told so many different things, all equally adamantly, about how Tabbouleh should be made – the length of time the burghul should be left to soak (the longer the soaking, the softer it will become; the fineness of the burghul also comes into play); what the proportion of burghul to parsley should be; whether mint should be included and, if so, how much; the amount of spring onions, oil and lemon juice, whether tomatoes should be in the salad as well as on top, and so on. Thus I have concluded that the only right thing to do is to make it the way you like it. Then, at least you will be happy. However, there are two practical points you may find useful: if you chop the herbs in a food processor, use the pulse action to avoid turning them to sludge, and if incorporating tomatoes, do not do so too far in advance.

50 G (2 OZ) BURGHUL

4 TABLESPOONS LEMON JUICE

4 TABLESPOONS OLIVE OIL

75 G (3 OZ) FLAT-LEAVED PARSLEY, FINELY CHOPPED

3-4 TABLESPOONS FINELY CHOPPED MINT (OPTIONAL)

5 SPRING ONIONS, FINELY CHOPPED

3 SUN-RIPENED TOMATOES, DESEEDED AND DICED

SALT AND PEPPER

INNER LEAVES OF CRISP LETTUCE TO SERVE

BLACK OLIVES TO GARNISH

Pour enough water over the burghul to cover it and leave for 15 minutes. Drain through a sieve then squeeze out the excess moisture. Tip into a bowl. Stir in the lemon juice and oil and salt and pepper. Leave until plump and tender.

Mix the herbs then stir into the burghul with the spring onions and tomatoes. Adjust the seasoning and quantity of lemon juice if necessary. Serve on a large flat serving dish lined with lettuce and garnish with black olives.

Serves 4

DOLMADES

Popular throughout the eastern Mediterranean, Dolmades (stuffed vine leaves) may be served hot or cold and may contain meat, or be meatless as in this recipe. Fresh leaves are sometimes available from Greek and Cypriot shops. If using leaves packed in brine, rinse them well, then blanch in boiling water for 3 minutes and drain well.

55 G (2¼ OZ) LONG GRAIN RICE

175 ML (6 FL OZ) BOILING WATER

12 FRESH VINE LEAVES

1½ TABLESPOONS OLIVE OIL

1 SMALL ONION, CHOPPED

25 G (1 OZ) PINE NUTS

500 G (1 LB) SUN-RIPENED TOMATOES, SKINNED, DESEEDED AND CHOPPED

1-2 TEASPOONS TOMATO PUREE

1 TABLESPOON CHOPPED PARSLEY

1 TABLESPOON CHOPPED MINT

¼ TEASPOON GROUND CINNAMON

3 CLOVES OF GARLIC, CRUSHED

2 TABLESPOONS LEMON JUICE

1 TABLESPOON CHOPPED OREGANO

SALT AND PEPPER

Cook rice in the boiling salted water in a covered pan for 12-15 minutes until tender and the liquid has been absorbed.

Meanwhile, blanch the vine leaves, in batches, in plenty of boiling water for 30 seconds, then turn them over. Drain in a colander, rinse under cold running water, then spread out each leaf, vein-side uppermost.

Heat the oil in a frying pan, add the onion and pine nuts and cook, stirring, until browned. Stir in the cooked rice, one third of the tomatoes, the tomato purée, parsley, mint, cinnamon and 2 garlic cloves for a couple of minutes. Stir in the lemon juice and seasoning, remove from the heat.

Place half the remaining tomatoes in a small flameproof casserole. Put a dessertspoon of the rice mixture on to the stalk end of a vine leaf, fold the sides over the filling, then roll up the leaf and press into a sausage shape. Place, seam-side down, in the casserole. Repeat with the remaining rice mixture and leaves, packing them into the casserole. Put the remaining tomatoes, garlic and oregano on top, season and place a suitable size plate on top to prevent the vine leaves unrolling during cooking. Cover the casserole, cook gently for 2 hours. Serve hot or cold with the juices spooned over.

Serves 6 as a first course, 4 as a main course

SIZZLING PRAWNS WITH GARLIC AND CHILLIES

The sound, as well as the smell, heralds the approach of a small cazuela of gambas al pil-pil, to use the onomatopoeic Spanish name. The generous amount of oil in which the prawns are cooked should still be actively sizzling when they are served, so that they stay crisp and dry. Each dish is carried to the table covered by a piece of bread, which serves the dual roles of stopping the oil spitting and providing a 'mop' for the flavoursome cooking juices.

100 ML (3½ FL OZ) OLIVE OIL

4-5 CLOVES OF GARLIC, FINELY CRUSHED

1 FRESH RED CHILLI, DESEEDED AND CHOPPED

500 G (1 LB) RAW PRAWNS, PEELED

2-3 TABLESPOONS CHOPPED PARSLEY

SEA SALT

TO SERVE

LEMON WEDGES

4 SLICES OF COUNTRY BREAD (SEE PAGE 113)

Heat the oil in 4 individual flameproof earthenware dishes over a high heat. Add the garlic and chilli, cook for 1-2 minutes, then add the prawns and sea salt.

Cook briskly for 2-3 minutes, shaking the dishes frequently. Stir in the parsley and serve the prawns at once accompanied by lemon wedges, and bread to mop up the juices.

Serves 4

MUSSELS WITH PROSCIUTTO

Although 'cozze' is the correct name for mussels, do not be surprised if, when in Liguria and Venezia Giulia, a shellfish called 'mitili' turns out to be mussels. The same applies to 'muscoli' in the Marches (and possibly elsewhere), and 'peoci' around Venice, from where this recipe comes. 1 kg (2 lb) mussels, scrubbed and debearded.

2 SUN-RIPENED TOMATOES, SKINNED, DESEEDED AND

FINELY CHOPPED

4 TABLESPOONS FINELY CHOPPED PROSCIUTTO

2 TABLESPOONS FINELY CHOPPED PARSLEY

1 CLOVE OF GARLIC, FINELY CHOPPED

PINCH OF PAPRIKA

APPROXIMATELY 2 TABLESPOONS DRY BREADCRUMBS

2 TABLESPOONS VIRGIN OLIVE OIL

COOKING LIQUID (OPTIONAL)

4 CLOVES OF GARLIC, FINELY CHOPPED

½ TEASPOON CRUSHED DRIED RED PEPPER FLAKES

5 TABLESPOONS FINELY CHOPPED PARSLEY

5 TABLESPOONS VIRGIN OLIVE OIL

125 ML (4 FL OZ) MEDIUM-BODIED DRY WHITE WINE

If making the cooking liquid, cook the garlic, crushed red pepper flakes and parsley in the oil in a large saucepan over a medium heat until the garlic is fragrant. Add the wine and mussels, cover and cook for 4-5 minutes, shaking the pan occasionally, until the mussels open; discard any mussels that remain closed.

If not making the cooking liquid, simply cook the mussels in 4 tablespoons water in a saucepan.

Twist off the top shells, leaving the mussels in the lower shells. Place on a rack in a large baking dish.

In a small bowl, combine the tomatoes, prosciutto, parsley, garlic and paprika. Divide between the mussels. Top each with a pinch of breadcrumbs, then trickle olive oil over them. Bake in a preheated oven, 200°C (400°F), Gas Mark 6, for 5 minutes. Serve with the cooking juices, if made.

Serves 6-8 as a first course

Left: Sizzling Prawns with Garlic and Chillies
Right: Mussels with Prosciutto

STUFFED KIBBEH

Serve hot or cold with a green salad, yogurt and flat bread.

250 G (8 OZ) FINE BURGHUL

½ LARGE ONION

500 G (1 LB) LEAN TENDER LAMB, SUCH AS LEG,

DICED AND CHILLED

APPROXIMATELY ½ TEASPOON GROUND ALLSPICE

APPROXIMATELY ½ TEASPOON PEPPER

APPROXIMATELY 4 TABLESPOONS ICED WATER

OLIVE OIL FOR DEEP FRYING

SALT

FILLING

2 TABLESPOONS OIL

1 ONION, FINELY CHOPPED

3 TABLESPOONS PINE NUTS

250 G (8 OZ) LEAN LAMB, MINCED

½ TEASPOON ALLSPICE

1 TEASPOON GROUND CINNAMON

1 TABLESPOON EACH CHOPPED PARSLEY AND MINT

SALT AND PEPPER

Soak the burghul in cold water for 20 minutes. Drain and squeeze out the excess moisture. Using a food processor, finely chop the onion. Add the diced lamb and allspice, season and mix together. Add the burghul, mix again to a smooth, soft texture. To check the level of spicing, fry a very small piece and taste it. Knead the mixture well by hand.

To make the filling, heat the oil, add the onion and cook, stirring occasionally, until soft and becoming golden. Add the pine nuts and fry until golden. Stir in the minced lamb and cook, stirring occasionally, until the lamb has changed colour and the juices evaporated. Add the remaining ingredients.

With oiled or wetted hands, take a piece of the kibbeh mixture about the size of an egg and form it into an egg shape. Holding it in the palm of one hand, make a small hole in it with the forefinger of the other hand and mould the kibbeh around and up the finger to make an oval shape with fairly thin walls. If the kibbeh cracks, repair it with a wetted finger – there must be no holes. Remove your finger.

Fill shell with about 1 tablespoon of the filling, then wet the rim of the opening and stick the edges together. Mould to a pointed oval. Repeat with remaining kibbeh and filling.

Deep fry a few at a time in preheated oil, 180-190°C (350-375°F), for about 4 minutes until an even rich dark brown. Drain on kitchen paper.

Serves 4

CHICKEN STRIPS WITH FRESH MINT

In the eastern and southern Mediterranean countries, both fresh and dried spearmint (the variety of mint most often used) is popular. Usually it is home-dried in the hot sun and dry atmosphere; the dried leaves are rubbed between the hands so their warmth releases the herb's flavouring oils.

2 TABLESPOONS LEMON JUICE

1½ TEASPOONS OLIVE OIL

2 TABLESPOONS CHOPPED FRESH MINT OR

1 TABLESPOON DRIED MINT

2 CLOVES OF GARLIC, FINELY CHOPPED

425 G (14 OZ) SKINLESS CHICKEN BREAST,

CUT ACROSS THE GRAIN INTO 1 CM (½ INCH) THICK SLICES

SALT AND PEPPER

LETTUCE LEAVES TO SERVE

TOMATO WEDGES TO GARNISH

In a large shallow dish, combine the lemon juice, olive oil, mint, garlic and seasonings. Add the chicken, turn to coat with the lemon mixture, cover and leave for up to 2 hours at room temperature or up to 8 hours in the refrigerator. Return to room temperature 30 minutes before cooking.

If using wooden skewers, soak 4 or 5 that are 15 cm (6 inches) long in water for 30 minutes. Thread the pieces of chicken on to skewers, then cook under a preheated grill or on a barbecue for 2½-3½ minutes each side. Serve on a bed of lettuce, garnished with tomato wedges.

Serves 4

ROAST VEGETABLE SALAD

*All around the Mediterranean there is a tradition of cooking
in the open air. Roasting a wide range of vegetables –
onions, garlic, peppers, aubergines, courgettes, fennel,
artichokes and so on – over the embers of a charcoal fire to
give them a subdued complexity, deep, seductive smoky
taste and silky texture is a high point of this way of
cooking. Elsewhere most of us have to resort to baking the
vegetables in the oven, and although the flavour will not be
quite so beguiling, it is nevertheless very good.*

2 SPANISH ONIONS, UNPEELED

500 G (1 LB) SMALL AUBERGINES

2 RED PEPPERS

3 FIRM BUT RIPE LARGE TOMATOES

8 CLOVES OF GARLIC

10 G (⅓ OZ) CUMIN SEEDS

3 TABLESPOONS LEMON JUICE

4 TABLESPOONS VIRGIN OLIVE OIL

3 TABLESPOONS WHITE WINE VINEGAR

2 TABLESPOONS FINELY CHOPPED PARSLEY OR TORN BASIL

SALT

Place the onions on a baking sheet and bake in a preheated
oven, 180°C (350°F), Gas Mark 4 for 10 minutes. Add the
aubergines and bake for a further 10 minutes. Add the
peppers and bake for 10 minutes before adding the tomatoes
and 6 of the garlic cloves. Cook for a further 15 minutes,
until all the vegetables are tender. If necessary, remove any
vegetables that have cooked more quickly than the others.
When the vegetables are cool enough to handle, peel them
with your fingers.

Cut the cores and seeds from the peppers and cut the
flesh into strips. Halve the tomatoes, discard the seeds and
slice the flesh. Slice the aubergines into strips and the onions
into rings. Arrange the peppers, tomatoes, aubergines and
onions in a serving dish.

Using a pestle and mortar or the end of a rolling pin in a
small bowl, pound the roasted and raw garlic and the cumin
seeds to a paste. Gradually beat in the lemon juice, oil and
vinegar, then add salt to taste. Pour over the vegetables and
sprinkle with parsley or basil. Serve warm or cold.

Serves 4

LAMBS' KIDNEYS
IN SHERRY

*Given the extent to which the recipe is known abroad,
kidneys cooked with sherry is not served in tapas bars so
often as might be expected. This is because the Spanish
know that, to be worth eating, the dish must be freshly and
quickly cooked with a deft hand – then it is truly delicious.
These quantities serve 4 for tapas, but only 2-3 if you turn
them into a meal and serve the dish with some good bread.*

500 G (1 LB) LAMBS' KIDNEYS

3 TABLESPOONS OLIVE OIL

2 CLOVES OF GARLIC, CHOPPED

125 G (4 OZ) MUSHROOMS, CHOPPED

50 G (2 OZ) SERRANO HAM, CHOPPED

6-8 TABLESPOONS FINO SHERRY

SALT AND PEPPER

CHOPPED PARSLEY TO GARNISH

Remove the fine skin from the outside of each kidney, cut
them in half lengthways and snip out and discard the cores.
Quarter each kidney, then set aside.

Heat the oil in a frying pan, add the garlic and cook for
2-3 minutes, stirring occasionally. Stir in the mushrooms and
fry until the liquid from the mushrooms has evaporated.

Stir the kidneys and ham into the pan and fry for
2-3 minutes, stirring frequently, so the kidneys are lightly
browned on the outside but still pink in the centre. Add the
sherry and seasonings and boil, stirring occasionally, until the
sherry has almost evaporated. Serve hot garnished with
chopped parsley.

Serves 4

Eggs & Cheese

Eggs are used extensively in Mediterranean cooking in various forms – deep-fried, roasted, hard-boiled or added to casseroles. Alternatively, they may be scrambled with other ingredients or cooked with vegetables, ham, spicy sausage or cheese as a type of omelette such as a tortilla or frittata. The shortage of cattle in much of the region means that cheeses are more often made from ewes', goats' or water buffaloes' milk, and are, therefore, comparatively less plentiful.

AUBERGINE AND CHEESE SANDWICHES

The smell of a batch of these cooking drew me to a stall in Istanbul's fish market, where a boy, about 16 years old, was forming the 'sandwiches', tossing them into the blackened pan of hot oil and always retrieving the right ones at the right moment, with all the aplomb of a seasoned expert. Anari is a Turkish whey cheese similar to ricotta; Mizithra a farmhouse-made, soft goats' or ewes' milk cheese.

1 AUBERGINE WEIGHING 375 G (12 OZ), CUT INTO

5 MM (¼ INCH) ROUND SLICES

125 G (4 OZ) ANARI OR MIZITHRA CHEESE, RICOTTA OR CREAM CHEESE

15 G (½ OZ) KEFALOTIRI OR PARMESAN CHEESE, FRESHLY GRATED

½ CLOVE OF GARLIC, CRUSHED

2 EGGS, BEATEN (SEPARATELY)

1½ TABLESPOONS CHOPPED MIXED HERBS SUCH AS PARSLEY,

MINT, DILL AND CHIVES

OLIVE OIL FOR COOKING

50 G (2 OZ) TOASTED BREADCRUMBS

SALT AND PEPPER

Sprinkle the aubergine slices with salt and leave in a colander for 30-60 minutes to drain. Rinse the slices and dry well.

Mash the cheeses and garlic with one of the beaten eggs, then mix in the herbs and seasonings.

Brush the aubergine slices with oil and cook under a preheated grill until browned. Drain on kitchen paper.

Cut each aubergine slice in half. Spread the cheese mixture on half of these then cover neatly with the remaining halves and press lightly together.

Put the toasted breadcrumbs into a shallow dish and the remaining beaten egg into a bowl. Dip the aubergine 'sandwiches' in the egg, allow excess to drain off and coat evenly with breadcrumbs.

Fry in hot olive oil for about 1½ minutes each side, until golden and crisp. Drain the 'sandwiches' on kitchen paper and serve hot garnished with finely chopped herbs such as dill, or parsley and mint.

Serves 3-4

FRIED MANCHEGO CHEESE FRITTERS

When these fritters are made with good Manchego cheese, properly fried and freshly cooked so that they are crisp and deliciously savoury, I find them extremely difficult to resist. Manchego is sometimes referred to as the Spanish equivalent of Cheddar, but it is more like Parmesan, as it, too, is made from ewes' milk, and rivals the Italian cheese for superiority when well made and matured.

OLIVE OIL FOR DEEP FRYING

2 EGG WHITES

125 G (4 OZ) MATURE MANCHEGO CHEESE, FINELY GRATED

50 G (2 OZ) FRESH BREADCRUMBS

ABOUT 1 TABLESPOON FINELY CHOPPED FRESH HERBS SUCH AS PARSLEY,

CHIVES AND THYME

PAPRIKA

SALT AND PEPPER

Heat a deep-fryer two thirds full with olive oil to 180-190°C (350-375°F).

Meanwhile, in a clean bowl, whisk the egg whites until stiff but not dry. Using a large metal spoon, lightly fold in the grated cheese, breadcrumbs and herbs. Season with salt, pepper and paprika.

Form the cheese mixture into small walnut-sized balls, adding the balls to the hot oil in the deep-fryer as they are shaped, but do not overcrowd the pan. Fry for about 3 minutes, until golden.

When cooked transfer the fritters to kitchen paper to drain. Serve hot.

Serves 4

Overleaf:
From left to right: Aubergine and Cheese Sandwiches, Fried Manchego Cheese Fritters and Basil and Cheese Frittata

BASIL AND CHEESE FRITTATA

With just fragrant basil and good Parmesan cheese, this most simple of frittata recipes is possibly my favourite.

7 EGGS

3 TABLESPOONS FRESHLY GRATED PARMESAN CHEESE

4 TABLESPOONS TORN BASIL LEAVES

40 G (1½ OZ) UNSALTED BUTTER

SALT AND PEPPER

Using a fork, lightly beat the eggs with the cheese, basil, salt and pepper until the yolks and whites are blended.

Heat the butter in a 30 cm (12 inch) heavy frying pan over a moderate heat until it begins to foam. Pour in the eggs and reduce the heat to very low. Cook very gently for about 15 minutes until the bulk is almost set, with only the top of the frittata still creamy and moist. Place under a preheated grill for 30-60 seconds until just set.

Loosen the edges of the frittata with a spatula and slide it on to a warm plate. Serve cut into wedges.

Serves 4

Variations
Asparagus Frittata – use 6 eggs and 50 g (2 oz) Parmesan cheese. Omit the basil, but add 500 g (1 lb) cooked asparagus cut into 1 cm (½ inch) lengths.
Courgette Eggah – salt 5 coarsely grated courgettes, drain in a colander for 30-60 minutes, then rinse and dry. Cook a chopped onion gently in olive oil in a 10 inch (25 cm) frying pan until very soft and golden. Add 1 crushed garlic clove, cook until aromatic, then stir in the courgettes and cook over a moderate heat, stirring until tender. Pour in 5 lightly beaten eggs, approximately 3 tablespoons chopped dill, and pepper, then cook as above.
Spinach Eggah – cook and drain 500 g (1 lb) fresh spinach or 250 g (8 oz) thawed frozen spinach. Lightly mix with 6 eggs, freshly grated nutmeg and salt and pepper. Cook as above in 50 g (2 oz) butter in a 30 cm (12 inch) frying pan.

HAMINE EGGS WITH FUL MEDAMES

Hamine Eggs have a unique flavour and creamy consistency that results from long, slow cooking. Onion skins added to the cooking water colour the eggs fawn. They are traditionally served with Ful Medames, made from a type of small dried broad bean which is a speciality of Egypt.

HAMINE EGGS

4 EGGS

SKINS OF 3-4 LARGE ONIONS

FUL MEDAMES

250 G (8 OZ) DRIED FUL BEANS, SOAKED OVERNIGHT

JUST COVERED BY COLD WATER

3 TABLESPOONS OLIVE OIL

3 CLOVES OF GARLIC, FINELY CHOPPED

1½ TABLESPOONS CHOPPED PARSLEY OR CORIANDER

2-3 TABLESPOONS LEMON JUICE

4 SPRING ONIONS, WHITE PART ONLY, CHOPPED

SALT AND PEPPER

TO SERVE

CHOPPED PARSLEY

LEMON JUICE

OLIVE OIL

For the hamine eggs, put the eggs and onion skins in a large saucepan. Cover generously with water, bring slowly to the boil, cover and simmer gently for 5-6 hours, or overnight. Keep an eye on the water level to ensure eggs are always covered – a layer of oil poured over the surface of the water will slow down the evaporation. A slow cooker is useful.

Drain the eggs and shell when cool enough to handle.

Meanwhile, drain the beans, put them into a heavy casserole or saucepan, just cover with water, cover the casserole or pan tightly and simmer very gently for 5-6 hours, or until tender. If the beans become too dry during cooking, pour in a little water but do not stir; at the end of cooking there should be hardly any spare liquid.

Tip the beans into a bowl, stir in the oil, garlic, parsley or coriander, lemon juice, salt and pepper. Leave to cool then stir in the spring onions. Serve in soup bowls with the eggs on top, and sprinkled with parsley. Traditionally each person crushes their bowlful of beans and eggs with a fork, mixing them together and adding extra lemon juice, olive oil and seasoning to taste.

Serves 4

MARINATED BALLS OF LABNE

Labne, laban, labna or labneh is Middle Eastern strained yogurt, traditionally made from ewes' or water buffaloes' milk. It is popular for breakfast spread on to opened out pitta bread, or as a mezze, when it is seasoned with salt and pepper or paprika and sprinkled with dill or mint, before being spread on pitta bread, trickled with oil and eaten with olives. It is also rolled into balls, packed into jars and covered with olive oil. I often flavour the balls with paprika or finely chopped mint, coriander, parsley, dill, or a mixture. Alternatively, sprigs of herbs, and/or a couple of split cloves of garlic can be added to the jar with the oil.

1-1½ TEASPOONS SALT

900 ML (1½ PINTS) YOGURT MADE FROM EWES' MILK

OR FULL-CREAM COWS' MILK

OLIVE OIL (OPTIONAL)

To make labne, stir the salt into the yogurt. Spoon it into the centre of a double thickness of muslin or piece of fine cotton, gather up the corners of the muslin or cloth, tie them securely and suspend over a bowl. Leave in a cool place to drain for at least 10 hours.

When the yogurt has reached the consistency of ricotta cheese, scoop up spoonfuls and roll them into smooth balls. Leave in the refrigerator for several hours until firm and a little dried. (If you are not making balls of labne, simply transfer it to a bowl or pots, cover and refrigerate.)

Pack the labne balls into a clean jar and cover with olive oil. Close the jar tightly and store at room temperature. If serving as a mezze, serve the balls in a bowl with a little of the oil, so that it can be used to soften the cheese.

The labne balls can be kept for up to 3 weeks.

Serves 4

Variation

Marinated Goats' Cheese – put 6 small, firm, but not dry goats' cheeses in a wide-necked jar with 1 tablespoon peppercorns, 2 small dried red chillies, 4 bay leaves and 3 sprigs of thyme. Cover with olive oil, close the jar and leave for 1-2 weeks; the longer the cheeses are left the stronger the flavour will become and the harder they will get. Eat within 3 months.

CHAKCHOUKA

The inclusion of hot red chillies pinpoints this, the most spicy of the egg dishes, as Tunisian.

3 TABLESPOONS OLIVE OIL

1 SPANISH ONION, THINLY SLICED

375 G (12 OZ) RED PEPPERS, CORED, DESEEDED AND SLICED

1-2 FRESH RED CHILLIES, DESEEDED AND CHOPPED

750 G (1½ LB) RIPE TOMATOES, SKINNED, DESEEDED AND CHOPPED

PINCH OF SUGAR (OPTIONAL)

4 EGGS

SALT AND PEPPER

Heat the oil in a deep heavy frying or sauté pan, add the onion and cook gently until it softens and begins to colour. Add the peppers and chillies and cook, stirring occasionally, until almost soft. Stir in the tomatoes and cook for a further 8 minutes or so until all the vegetables are soft but the mixture has not become a mush. Add salt and pepper and a little sugar, if necessary.

Make 4 deep depressions in the vegetable mixture, break in the eggs, cover the pan and cook gently until the eggs are set to the required degree, basting once or twice with the juices. Serve immediately.

Serves 4

Variation

Huevos a la Flamenca – cook ½ a finely chopped Spanish onion and 2 cloves of crushed garlic until soft. Add 2 slices of chopped serrano ham and 1 chopped red pepper, cook for 2 minutes, then add 1 teaspoon paprika. After 30 seconds, stir in 2 skinned, deseeded and chopped tomatoes. Simmer to a thickish purée. Add 75 g (3 oz) cooked fresh or frozen peas, 125 g (4 oz) cooked green beans and a little tomato purée if necessary. Season. Pour into a shallow ovenproof dish or 4 individual dishes. Form 4 shallow depressions and break an egg into each. Scatter over 2 slices chopped serrano ham and lay a chorizo slice on the yolks. Cook in a preheated oven, 230°C (450°F), Gas Mark 8, for 8-10 minutes for whites that are just set but with still moist yolks. Cook for 15 minutes for firmer eggs. Sprinkle over a little parsley.

From left to right:
Hamine Eggs with Ful Medames,
Marinated Balls of Labne and Chakchouka

PIPERADE

The regional pepper to use for Piperade is the 'piment d'Espelletes', grown around the town of the same name in the Pays Basque, and the centre for the cultivation of several varieties of sweetish or hottish red peppers and in the business of sun-drying and selling them. The ham can be fried if preferred and the eggs mixed with all the vegetables. Serve for a light main course, a snack or supper dish, especially in summer.

4 THIN SLICES OF BAYONNE HAM

2 TABLESPOONS OLIVE OIL

1 SPANISH ONION, CHOPPED

2 CLOVES OF GARLIC, CHOPPED

1 GREEN PEPPER, CHARRED, CORED, DESEEDED AND SLICED

1 RED PEPPER, CHARRED, CORED, DESEEDED AND SLICED

750 G (1½ LB) VERY RIPE TOMATOES, SKINNED,

DESEEDED AND CHOPPED

6-8 EGGS

SALT AND PEPPER

Trim the fat from the ham. Reserve the ham, dice the fat and heat with the oil in a heavy-bottomed frying pan. Add the onion and garlic and cook, stirring occasionally, until softened but not coloured. Stir in the peppers and tomatoes, season and simmer gently for about 15 minutes, stirring occasionally, until lightly thickened. Transfer two thirds of the vegetables to a saucepan, cover and keep warm. Place the slices of ham under a low grill to warm.

Stir the eggs into the frying pan and cook over a low heat, stirring gently, until the eggs begin to thicken. Remove immediately from the heat. Place a slice of ham in each of 4 warm deep plates, place a quarter of the vegetable mixture on top, add the egg mixture and serve immediately.

Serves 4

MENEMEN

Menemen takes its name from a small coastal town in western Turkey. 'Sivri biber' are the best peppers to use – long and pale with thin, moderately hot tasting flesh. I have seen them in shops selling Turkish foods in this country, but if you are unable to buy them, use milder green chillies or a mixture of ordinary green peppers and hot green chillies. Sometimes 'beyaz peynir', the local feta cheese, which is softer than those we usually get here, is sprinkled over the mixture when it is almost ready to give a more savoury and sustaining dish; then a scattering of parsley finishes the dish.

2 TABLESPOONS OIL

125 G (4 OZ) SWEET GREEN PEPPER, OR A COMBINATION OF SWEET

AND CHILLI PEPPERS, CORED, DESEEDED AND FINELY CHOPPED

2 LARGE, VERY RIPE YET FIRM TOMATOES, SKINNED,

DESEEDED AND CHOPPED

4 EGGS, BEATEN

SALT

WARM PITTA BREAD TO SERVE

Heat the oil in a small frying pan, add the pepper and chilli, if used, and the tomatoes and cook over a moderate heat for 5-6 minutes until the pepper has relaxed and the tomato has begun to dry out. Sprinkle with salt.

Lower the heat, stir in the beaten eggs and continue to stir gently until the eggs are beginning to set but are still creamy. Serve the Menemen immediately with warm pitta bread to mop up the juices.

Serves 2

EGGS IN SPINACH

Served with a tomato or red pepper salad and crusty bread, this Turkish recipe makes a tasty lunch or supper dish. A lighter, less savoury version can be made by omitting the cheese and, instead, sprinkling a little olive oil over each uncooked egg, then serving with thick yogurt. To serve as a first course, you could use individual flameproof earthenware dishes, such as cazuelas, or divide the spinach mixture between 4 ovenproof dishes, break the eggs into these and bake in a preheated oven, 180°C (350°F), Gas Mark 4, for about 15 minutes until the eggs are set to the firmness you like.

500 G (1 LB) FRESH SPINACH, STALKS REMOVED

2 TABLESPOONS OLIVE OIL

1 ONION, FINELY CHOPPED

1 CLOVE OF GARLIC, FINELY CHOPPED

4 EGGS

75-125 G (3-4 OZ) FETA CHEESE

SALT AND PEPPER

CHOPPED WHITE AND GREEN PARTS OF SPRING ONIONS,

OR PAPRIKA TO SERVE

Wash and drain, but do not dry the spinach. Shred it and place in a large saucepan. Heat, stirring occasionally, until it is wilted and there is no spare liquid visible. Tip into a colander and press to extract as much liquid as possible.

Heat the oil in a heavy frying pan and cook the onion until transparent and lightly browned, add the garlic. Stir in the spinach towards the end of cooking and keep stirring for a few minutes. Season with pepper and a very little salt, depending on the saltiness of the cheese.

With the back of a spoon make 4 hollows in the spinach mixture. Break an egg into each depression. Crumble the cheese over the entire surface and grind over black pepper. Heat over a medium heat until steaming, then cover with a lid and leave for 5-10 minutes until the eggs are set to the required degree. Sprinkle with chopped spring onions or paprika. Serve hot or warm.

Serves 2

FRIED CHEESE AND EGGS

In Greece the recipe is named after the dish in which it is cooked and served – saganaki. In the ouzeries, one large slice of cheese is fried in a saganaki and served individually at table. There, hard dry Kashkaval or Kasseri cheese is used; in Sicily, I have been served fried Pecorino Sardo cheese and eggs and no doubt, other cheeses are given the same treatment. The oil may be flavoured by frying garlic and/or dried red chilli in it first, if liked.

4 FINGER-THICK SLICES OF HARD CHEESE SUCH AS KASSERI OR PECORINO

2 TABLESPOONS OLIVE OIL

4 EGGS

SALT AND PEPPER

Fry the cheese in hot oil in a heavy frying pan just large enough to hold the 4 slices. When the cheese begins to melt and bubble, break an egg over each slice and continue to cook until the white has set. Serve immediately, sprinkled with salt and pepper.
Serves 4

Variation

Cut thick slices from a block of halumi cheese and pat dry with kitchen paper. Marinate in olive oil with thyme or coriander and pepper for at least 30 minutes, before frying in the marinating oil.

To give the cheese a crisp coating, and also prevent cheese that is not sufficiently hard from melting too quickly, press polenta into the slices before frying. Fry the eggs in a separate pan then serve on top of the cheese. With this variation, mozzarella cheese can be used.

Vegetables & Salads

Vegetables are the glory of the Mediterranean diet – bought with care and close scrutiny, cherished, treated with respect and eaten with relish. The rich repertoire of varied and well-flavoured dishes, enhanced by the skilful use of herbs, spices and other flavourings, includes vegetables that are grilled, boiled, deep-fried, stuffed, baked, added to omelettes, tarts and pies, transformed into richly flavoured, colourful casseroles, or tossed with dressings and served as warm or cold salads.

WARM SALADE NICOISE

It is impossible to give a definitive recipe for Salade Niçoise as there is a lot of controversy over what can and cannot be included in an authentic one. This one will be greeted with horror by any traditionalists, but I've included it not just to be contentious, but because it makes a very good dish, and one that is far better than many a so-called Salade Niçoise.

ABOUT 250 G (8 OZ) SMALL NEW POTATOES, SCRUBBED,

OR MEDIUM POTATOES, SCRUBBED AND QUARTERED

5 TABLESPOONS VIRGIN OLIVE OIL

2 TABLESPOONS RED WINE VINEGAR

250 G (8 OZ) FRENCH BEANS, TOPPED AND TAILED

250 G (8 OZ) FRESH TUNA STEAK, CUT INTO FINGER STRIPS

2 CLOVES OF GARLIC, FINELY CHOPPED

2 ANCHOVY FILLETS, CHOPPED

APPROXIMATELY 1½ TEASPOONS DIJON MUSTARD

1 RED PEPPER, CHARRED, SKINNED, DESEEDED AND THINLY SLICED

2 TABLESPOONS CAPERS

SALT AND PEPPER

LEMON WEDGES TO SERVE (OPTIONAL)

Steam the potatoes for 8-10 minutes, until just tender. Transfer to a serving bowl and toss gently with 1 tablespoon each of the oil and the vinegar, and salt and pepper.

Steam the French beans for 5-6 minutes until just tender. Set aside.

Heat 1 tablespoon of the oil in a non-stick frying pan, add the tuna and sear evenly over a high heat. Add to the potato mixture. Add the remaining oil to the frying pan, then stir in the garlic and anchovies for 30 seconds. Stir in the remaining vinegar and boil for 1 minute or so. Stir in the mustard, then pour over the potato mixture. Add the pepper strips, beans, capers and more black pepper. Toss gently, taste and adjust the flavourings if necessary, then serve immediately with lemon wedges, if liked.

Serves 2 as a main course

MUSHROOM AND CHEESE SALAD

In some versions of the recipe, the mushrooms are marinated in oil and vinegar or lemon juice; in others, olive oil alone is used, while other recipes merely sprinkle sliced mushrooms with oil. If you use lemon juice or vinegar, be sure to balance it against the oil so that there is just enough acidity to give the salad the sharpness it needs to contrast with the mushrooms. It is also important not to swamp the salad with dressing. The texture and flavour of porcini (ceps) really do make quite a difference, but, of course, money and season do not always permit such perfection so, on these occasions, I recommend substituting oyster or brown cap mushrooms. Serve as an antipasto, a simple lunch or with poultry or white meat.

300 G (10 OZ) PORCINI (CEPS), OYSTER OR LARGE BROWN

CAP MUSHROOMS, THINLY SLICED

65 G (2½ OZ) PARMESAN CHEESE, SHAVED

10 BASIL LEAVES, TORN

3 TABLESPOONS OLIVE OIL

1 TABLESPOON LEMON JUICE OR WHITE WINE VINEGAR

SALT AND PEPPER

Arrange the mushrooms on a large serving plate. Scatter over the cheese, then the basil.

Whisk together the oil, lemon juice or vinegar and salt and pepper and pour evenly over the salad. Serve at once or leave for 30 minutes.

Serves 4

Variation

Broad Bean and Pecorino Salad – blanch 1.5 kg (3 lb) fresh shelled broad beans in boiling salted water for 1 minute. Drain, then mix with 250 g (8 oz) diced Pecorino Romano, 3 tablespoons olive oil and black pepper.

Overleaf:
Left: Warm Salad Niçoise
Right: Mushroom and Cheese Salad

MOZZARELLA AND TOMATO SALAD

As the concept is simple and the basic ingredients readily available, this has become a very popular salad, especially with restaurants. However, whether it tastes any good rests entirely on the quality of the raw materials. On the island of its birth, Capri, where the salad is known as Caprese, really fresh buffalo mozzarella, sun-soaked, juicy tomatoes, rich olive oil and well-flavoured basil are used, and it can be a truly memorable salad – quite unlike the versions served elsewhere with rubbery cheese, tasteless, watery tomatoes and oil and basil that lack character. This is a salad to be eaten immediately or, at least, within 30 minutes. Although not quite the genuine Caprese, really good, pitted black olives and fat capers may also be scattered over.

150 G (5 OZ) VERY FRESH BUFFALO MOZZARELLA CHEESE, THICKLY SLICED

2-3 EXTRA LARGE TOMATOES, THICKLY SLICED

LEAVES FROM A LARGE BUNCH BASIL, TORN

EXTRA VIRGIN OLIVE OIL

SALT AND PEPPER

Arrange alternate slices of mozzarella cheese and tomato in circles on 4 small plates or 1 large one. Scatter over the torn basil leaves.

Season the olive oil with salt and black pepper and trickle over the salads.

Serves 4

GREEK COUNTRY SALAD

Greek tavernas worldwide serve what could be dubbed as Greece's national salad, Horiatiki Salata. Purists say that it should be made with two types of lettuce – cos and round, the former shredded, the latter torn. They should be tossed with oil in a large bowl, then the other ingredients carefully added in layers of contrasting colours. Finally, the dressing is trickled over the top. The bowl is then placed in the centre of the table and each person dips in their fork, taking what they fancy.

4 TABLESPOONS OLIVE OIL

1 TABLESPOON RED WINE VINEGAR

1 CLOVE OF GARLIC, CRUSHED

½ CUCUMBER, PEELED IF LIKED

1 SMALL ROUND LETTUCE, TORN

1 SMALL COS LETTUCE, SHREDDED

3 FIRM BUT RIPE TOMATOES, CUT INTO WEDGES

1 SPANISH ONION, THINLY SLICED INTO RINGS

1 GREEN PEPPER, CORED, DESEEDED AND THINLY SLICED INTO RINGS

150 G (5 OZ) FETA CHEESE, CRUMBLED

12 OR MORE BLACK KALAMATA OLIVES

12 TABLESPOONS COARSELY CHOPPED PARSLEY

2 TEASPOONS CHOPPED OREGANO

SALT AND PEPPER

Vigorously whisk together the oil, vinegar, garlic and salt and pepper. Leave for 1 hour.

Halve the cucumber lengthways, scoop out the seeds and thinly slice the cucumber. Sprinkle with salt and leave to drain. Rinse the cucumber and dry with kitchen paper.

Whisk the oil and vinegar again, then toss a little of it with the lettuces in a bowl. Layer the tomatoes, cucumber, onion, pepper, cheese and olives on the lettuce. Pour over the remaining dressing then scatter over the parsley and the oregano.

Serves 4

AUBERGINE CANNELLONI

The 'cannelloni' are formed from slices of aubergine cut along the length of the vegetable. They are filled with a simple, light mixture of soft goats' and ricotta cheeses flavoured with basil, then topped with a tomato sauce, to make a dish that is tasty and satisfying without being too heavy.

4 AUBERGINES, ABOUT 250 G (8 OZ) EACH

OLIVE OIL FOR BRUSHING

250 G (8 OZ) RICOTTA CHEESE

250 G (8 OZ) SOFT GOATS' CHEESE

125 G (4 OZ) PARMESAN CHEESE, FRESHLY GRATED

4 TABLESPOONS CHOPPED BASIL

SAUCE

2 TABLESPOONS OLIVE OIL

I ONION, CHOPPED

2 CLOVES OF GARLIC, CRUSHED

I KG (2 LB) SUN-RIPENED TOMATOES, SKINNED, DESEEDED AND CHOPPED

150 ML (¼ PINT) VEGETABLE OR CHICKEN STOCK, MEDIUM-BODIED DRY WHITE WINE, OR WATER

APPROXIMATELY I TABLESPOON SUN-DRIED TOMATO PUREE

SALT AND PEPPER

TO GARNISH

SHAVED PARMESAN CHEESE

BASIL SPRIGS

To make the sauce, heat the oil in a saucepan, add the onion and cook gently, stirring occasionally, until soft. Stir in the garlic, tomatoes, stock, wine or water, and tomato purée then simmer until thickened to a fairly light sauce. Season.

Meanwhile, thinly slice the aubergines lengthways and brush lightly with oil. Cook under a preheated grill until evenly browned on both sides. Drain on kitchen paper.

Mix together the cheeses, chopped basil and seasoning to taste. Spoon the cheese mixture along the aubergines and roll the slices, from the short end, around the filling. Place the rolls, seam-side down, in a single layer in a shallow baking dish and place in a preheated oven, 190°C (375°F), Gas Mark 5, for about 10-15 minutes, until the filling is hot. Reheat the sauce if necessary.

Divide the 'cannelloni' between warmed plates, spoon the sauce across the aubergine rolls, scatter over the shaved Parmesan cheese and garnish with basil sprigs.

Serves 6-8 as a first course, 4 as a main course

ARTICHOKE AND BROAD BEAN STEW

One of my strongest memories of Crete is driving late one evening, when the sun was a fast-sinking glowing ball, through endless eerie fields 'policed' by tall, stately, globe artichoke plants topped by their spiked caps. Next day, we lunched at a taverna just outside Fourfouras, which served artichokes in innumerable ways. We sat under the vines, nibbled home-pickled artichoke hearts and sipped ouzo while making our choice. I plumped for this dish of delicious home-grown artichokes and beans with rich cooking juices which came with thick slices of country bread.

4 ARTICHOKES

½ LEMON

4 TABLESPOONS VIRGIN OLIVE OIL, PLUS EXTRA FOR SPRINKLING

I SMALL ONION, FINELY CHOPPED

500 G (I LB) SHELLED FRESH SMALL BROAD BEANS (OR THAWED FROZEN BEANS)

APPROXIMATELY I½ TABLESPOONS CHOPPED MINT OR DILL

2 TABLESPOONS WATER

SALT AND PEPPER

TO SERVE (OPTIONAL)

CHOPPED PARSLEY

FRESHLY GRATED KEFALOTIRI CHEESE

Snap the stems from the artichokes and pull away the outer leaves to leave a cone of soft small leaves in the centre. Cut off the soft cone and cut away the hairy choke. Cut each bottom lengthways into quarters, then cut each quarter in half lengthways. Rub all the cut surfaces with the half lemon.

In a saucepan just large enough to hold the vegetables, heat the oil. Add the onion, cook for 2-3 minutes and then add the artichokes. Stir around for 4-5 minutes before covering and cooking over a moderate heat, shaking the pan occasionally, until the artichokes are almost half cooked, about 5 minutes. Add the fresh beans, mint or dill, water and seasoning, cover tightly and cook for about 10 minutes, depending on the age and size of the beans, shaking the pan occasionally, until the vegetables are tender. (If using frozen beans, add them when the artichokes are almost tender and cook for a further 4-5 minutes.)

Serve in warm, deep plates. Grind black pepper over the top, sprinkle with chopped parsley, a few drops of olive oil and a little cheese if liked.

Serves 4

Left: Aubergine Cannelloni
Right: Artichoke and Broad Bean Stew

RATATOUILLE

The name ratatouille is derived from two slang words –
'rata' in French army parlance means simple rations, and
'touiller' meaning to stir or mix. The flavour develops with
time and it is delicious with meats or poultry, grilled
polenta, poached eggs, tossed with pasta, as a filling for
omelettes, or if thick, for small savoury pastries.

2 AUBERGINES

3 COURGETTES, SLICED

7 TABLESPOONS OLIVE OIL

1 SPANISH ONION, VERY THINLY SLICED

3 CLOVES OF GARLIC, CRUSHED

2 LARGE RED PEPPERS, CORED, DESEEDED AND THINLY SLICED

4 LARGE SUN-RIPENED TOMATOES, SKINNED, DESEEDED AND CHOPPED

LEAVES FROM A FEW SPRIGS OF THYME, MARJORAM AND OREGANO

ABOUT 2 TABLESPOONS EACH OF CHOPPED PARSLEY AND TORN BASIL LEAVES

SALT AND PEPPER

Halve each aubergine lengthways and cut into slices about 2.5 cm (1 inch) thick. Sprinkle salt over the aubergine and courgette slices, place in a colander and leave for 1 hour. Rinse well then dry thoroughly with kitchen paper.

Heat 2 tablespoons of the oil in a heavy flameproof casserole, add the aubergine and sauté for a few minutes. Add another tablespoon of the oil and the onion and garlic and sauté for a few minutes. Add the red peppers and cook, stirring occasionally, for a minute or so. Add another 2 tablespoons of the oil and the courgettes. Cook, stirring occasionally, for a few minutes. Add the tomatoes, snip in the herb leaves, season lightly and add the remaining 2 tablespoons of oil. Cover the casserole and cook very gently for 30-40 minutes, stirring occasionally. Stir in the parsley and basil and cook, uncovered, for 5-10 minutes until there is no surplus liquid. Serve warm or cold.
Serves 4

Variation

Peperonata – soften 1 chopped onion and 2 chopped cloves of garlic in 4 tablespoons of oil in a large frying pan. Stir in 500 g (1 lb) skinned, deseeded and chopped extra large tomatoes and cook gently for 10-15 minutes until thickened. Stir in 4 charred, cored and sliced red peppers and cook for a further 5 minutes or so, until the peppers are soft. Add salt and pepper to taste and sugar if necessary to give a rich flavour. Cool for about 5 minutes before serving sprinkled with parsley.

BRAISED BROCCOLI WITH GARLIC

This old-fashioned, southern Italian way of cooking broccoli
slowly and gently produces a very different vegetable from
the one that is currently in vogue. Instead of being crisp,
the broccoli melts on the tongue, as does the garlic. Chillies
and sun-dried tomatoes or olives add a contrasting
piquancy that lifts the dish. Serve as a first course, an
accompaniment to a plain main course or for a light lunch
or supper dish.

750 G (1½ LB) BROCCOLI

4 TABLESPOONS OLIVE OIL

6 CLOVES OF GARLIC

2 DRIED RED CHILLIES, DESEEDED AND COARSELY CHOPPED

4 HALVES OF SUN-DRIED TOMATOES, OR 8 BLACK OLIVES, HALVED AND PITTED

250 ML (8 FL OZ) WHITE WINE OR WATER

40 G (1½ OZ) PECORINO ROMANO OR PARMESAN CHEESE, SHAVED THINLY

Trim the woody ends from the broccoli and discard. Leave slim pieces of broccoli whole, but slice thicker stems in half or quarters along their length.

Pour the oil into a wide heavy saucepan, stir in the broccoli, garlic, chillies and sun-dried tomatoes or olives. Add the wine or water, cover and cook over a low heat for 45-60 minutes until the liquid has almost completely evaporated; if necessary, uncover the pan towards the end.

Tip into a warm dish and scatter over the cheese.
Serves 4

SPICED CASSEROLE OF SWEET POTATOES AND PEAS

I have subdued the original flavourings of this Tunisian recipe so that the combination of lemon juice, honey, cinnamon and chillies subtly complements the flavour of sweet potatoes, but if you prefer a dish with a punchier flavour, increase their quantities.

4 TABLESPOONS LEMON JUICE

3-4 TEASPOONS CLEAR HONEY

I TEASPOON GROUND CINNAMON

¾ TEASPOON CHILLI POWDER, OR TO TASTE

2 TABLESPOONS OLIVE OIL

750 G (1½ LB) SWEET POTATOES, CUT INTO I CM (½ INCH) CUBES

I ONION, FINELY CHOPPED

2 CLOVES OF GARLIC, FINELY CHOPPED

4 TABLESPOONS WATER

SALT

Mix together I tablespoon of the lemon juice, all of the honey, cinnamon and chilli powder. Set aside.

Heat the oil in a large, heavy frying pan, add the sweet potatoes and cook, stirring occasionally, for 10 minutes. Add the onion, garlic, salt, remaining lemon juice and water. Cook, stirring occasionally, for about 5 minutes until the onion begins to brown. Add the spiced honey mixture, cook, stirring, for 2 minutes, then serve.

Serves 4

Variation

Tunisian Spiced Carrots – to serve hot or cold. Boil I kg (2lb) sliced young carrots for about 3 minutes. Drain. Soften I chopped onion and 2 cloves of garlic in olive oil. Add the carrots, 150 ml (¼ pint) vegetable or chicken stock, I teaspoon each clear honey, harissa, cumin and coriander and season. Cook for a further 10-12 minutes. Stir in chopped parsley before serving.

BRAISED FENNEL WITH CHEESE

In Florence, Italy, fennel used to be eaten at the end of the meal, as it was believed to help digestion and was therefore a fitting food with which to round off a heavy or rich meal. This practice has virtually vanished, with the exception of a few places in Tuscany, where sliced fennel is served as a digestif, sometimes with mandarins or other oranges. Nowadays, fennel appears frequently in baked vegetable dishes, including this one, which, though simple, is one of the best.

4 BULBS OF YOUNG FENNEL

3 TABLESPOONS LEMON JUICE

50 G (2 OZ) UNSALTED BUTTER, CUBED

I TABLESPOON VIRGIN OLIVE OIL

50 G (2 OZ) PARMESAN CHEESE, FRESHLY GRATED,

OR GORGONZOLA CHEESE, CRUMBLED

SALT AND PEPPER

BROWNED FLAKED ALMONDS, OR CHOPPED TOASTED WALNUTS TO GARNISH

Trim and reserve the feathery fennel fronds. Cut the fennel into quarters and boil in salted water to which the lemon juice has been added for about 15 minutes, until tender but still crisp. Drain through a colander and place on kitchen paper to drain further.

Place the fennel in a single layer in a baking dish, scatter over the butter and olive oil, sprinkle with the cheese, season with plenty of black pepper then place, uncovered, in a preheated oven, 200°C (400°F), Gas Mark 6, for about 20 minutes until brown. Serve with the nuts scattered over.

Serves 4

CATALAN SPINACH WITH RAISINS AND PINE NUTS

Pine nuts and raisins signal the Arab influence that lies behind this interesting Spanish treatment of spinach; the leaves of Swiss chard may also be cooked in this way. Serve as a vegetable accompaniment or as a first course accompanied by croûtons.

3 TABLESPOONS OLIVE OIL

40 G (1½ OZ) TOASTED PINE NUTS

750 G (1½ LB) FRESH SPINACH, STALKS REMOVED

1-2 CLOVES OF GARLIC, CHOPPED

40 G (1½ OZ) RAISINS

SALT AND PEPPER

Heat 1 tablespoon of the oil in a small saucepan, add the pine nuts and fry until golden. Using a slotted spoon, transfer to kitchen paper to drain.

Heat the remaining oil in a large saucepan. Wash, but do not dry the spinach, add to the pan with the garlic and cook over a high heat for about 5 minutes, stirring with a wooden spoon, until wilted and there is no excess moisture visible. Stir in the pine nuts, raisins and seasonings and cook for a couple of minutes.

Serves 4

From top to bottom: Tumbet,
Stuffed Onions and Catalan Spinach
with Raisins and Pine Nuts

TUMBET

My first experience of Tumbet was in Valldemossa, Majorca, where as hard-up students we each ate just a single dish of it, to the consternation of the restaurant proprietor, who considered it an accompaniment to a main dish of grilled meat. For us, however, Tumbet had the virtues of being cheap and filling as well as very tasty.

3 AUBERGINES

OLIVE OIL FOR COOKING

2 ONIONS, CHOPPED

3 CLOVES OF GARLIC, CRUSHED

4 LARGE SUN-RIPENED TOMATOES, SKINNED, DESEEDED AND CHOPPED

2-3 SPRIGS OF OREGANO OR MARJORAM

2 LARGE POTATOES, CUT INTO SLICES

SUGAR (OPTIONAL)

2 RED PEPPERS, CORED, DESEEDED AND SLICED

SALT AND PEPPER

CRUSTY BREAD TO SERVE

Quarter the aubergines lengthways, then halve each piece. Place in a colander, sprinkle evenly with salt and leave for 30-60 minutes to drain.

Heat about 2 tablespoons of oil, add the onions and garlic, fry gently until softened and lightly browned. Stir in the tomatoes, oregano or marjoram and simmer for about 15 minutes.

Meanwhile, heat a thin layer of oil in a large frying pan, add a single layer of potato slices and cook over a moderate heat until golden on both sides and about three-quarters cooked. Remove with a slotted spoon, drain on kitchen paper and put into a flameproof earthenware casserole. Repeat with the remaining potatoes.

Season the tomato sauce and add a little sugar if necessary. Pour about one third over the potatoes.

Rinse and dry the aubergine pieces and fry in batches in the frying pan until golden. Using a slotted spoon, transfer to kitchen paper to drain, then add to the casserole. Pour over another third of the tomato sauce.

Fry pepper slices in the pan and add to the casserole. Pour over the remaining sauce. Almost cover, leaving a small gap for steam to escape. Simmer very gently for 15-20 minutes until the potatoes are tender and the sauce thick.

Alternatively, bake, uncovered, in a preheated oven, 180°C (350°F), Gas Mark 4, for 15 minutes. Let stand for 5-10 minutes before serving or cool to room temperature. Serve with plenty of crusty bread to mop up the juices.

Serves 4

STUFFED ONIONS

One year I stayed with friends who have an old farmhouse in the foothills of the Pyrenees. One chilly Sunday morning we went to the open-air market set beneath a canopy of sycamore trees in Ceret, a favourite haunt of Picasso. We behaved like tourists, buying Catalan cotton espadrilles and yards of brightly coloured fabrics (which have still not been made into anything!), and eating cechi, the local cream-filled doughnuts fried to order, as we wandered. We also bought large loaves of wholemeal bread to eat with the stuffed onions we had left in the old, heavy oven. By the time we got home, the large onions had been rendered mellow, sweet, succulent and unforgettable by the long, slow cooking.

4 LARGE ONIONS, 300-375 G (10-12 OZ) EACH, UNPEELED

125 G (4 OZ) SOFT GOATS' CHEESE

4 SUN-DRIED TOMATOES, SOAKED IF NECESSARY, CHOPPED

2 EGG YOLKS

½ TEASPOON CRUMBLED THYME

2 TABLESPOONS CHOPPED PARSLEY

2 TABLESPOONS VIRGIN OLIVE OIL, PLUS EXTRA FOR THE DISH

PEPPER

Cook the onions in their skins in boiling salted water for 15 minutes. Drain then run cold water over them. When cool enough to handle, cut off and reserve the top quarter or so of each onion. Using a teaspoon or melon baller, carefully scoop out the centre of the onions, leaving a shell 2-3 layers thick. Sit these upright in an oiled baking dish.

Finely chop the centres and mix with the cheese, sun-dried tomatoes, egg yolks, herbs and plenty of pepper. Divide between the onion shells, replace the reserved tops, trickle over the olive oil and bake in a preheated oven, 180°C (350°F), Gas Mark 4, for 30-40 minutes, basting with the cooking juices towards the end. Serve warm or cold.
Serves 4 as first course, 2 as a main course

Variation
Substitute 8 pitted and chopped oil-cured black olives for the sun-dried tomatoes.

MUSHROOMS WITH TOMATOES AND ANCHOVY

Small amounts of anchovy fillets imbue foods with a subtle savoury flavour without imparting a detectable fishy taste, a trick canny Italians learned long ago. They also learned that it is a particularly effective way to enhance the taste of one of their most favourite foods, mushrooms.

4 TABLESPOONS OLIVE OIL

I LARGE CLOVE OF GARLIC, FINELY CHOPPED

500 G (I LB) MEDIUM CAP MUSHROOMS, PREFERABLY CHESTNUT, HALVED

2 SUN-RIPENED TOMATOES, SKINNED, DESEEDED AND CHOPPED

4 ANCHOVY FILLETS, RINSED IF NECESSARY, CHOPPED

2 TABLESPOONS CHOPPED PARSLEY

SALT AND PEPPER

Heat the oil in a frying pan, add the garlic and cook for 1 minute. Add the mushrooms and cook, stirring occasionally, for 10-15 minutes until the juices evaporate and the mushrooms are beginning to brown.

Stir in the tomatoes, anchovies, 1 tablespoon of the parsley and salt and pepper. Simmer for 5 minutes until lightly thickened.

Transfer to a serving dish and sprinkle with the remaining chopped parsley.
Serves 4

GENOESE MUSHROOMS AND POTATOES

This Ligurian recipe for potatoes with mushrooms is a clever way of making it appear as if there are more mushrooms than there are because the potatoes absorb the flavour of the mushrooms. The characteristic Ligurian touch of adding basil gives a final fillip to the dish. The mushrooms should really be fresh porcini (ceps), but as these are rarely available, I boost cultivated mushrooms, preferably chestnut (brown) ones, with dried ceps.

20 G (¾ OZ) DRIED CEPS

300 ML (½ PINT) HOT WATER

375 G (12 OZ) MUSHROOMS, THINLY SLICED

500 G (1 LB) POTATOES, THINLY SLICED

4 CLOVES OF GARLIC, CRUSHED

LEAVES FROM A BUNCH OF BASIL

OLIVE OIL FOR OILING THE DISH

SALT AND PEPPER

Soak the dried mushrooms in the hot water for 30 minutes. Drain off and strain the liquid through muslin or a filter paper. Simmer the reconstituted mushrooms in the liquid until the liquid has evaporated. Toss with the fresh mushrooms, potatoes, garlic, basil and seasoning.

Oil a baking dish that will hold the potatoes and mushrooms in a layer no more than about 4 cm (1½ inches) deep. Make an even layer of the mushroom mixture and bake in a preheated oven, 180°C (350°F), Gas Mark 4, for about 45 minutes until the potatoes are tender; turn the ingredients over about halfway through. Leave to stand for a couple of minutes before serving.

Serves 4

TURKISH STUFFED AUBERGINES

Stuffed aubergines are frequently called 'Immam bayeldi', which, in Turkish, means 'the sultan (or priest) fainted', supposedly at the amount of oil used in its making, but whether his swoon was from delight at the quality of the dish or horror at its cost is not known. I have seen so many different versions that I have no idea what the recipe the sultan ate was like, although to be in line with the legend, oil should be used lavishly. In this recipe it is not but you can add more oil if you like. A modification I like is to add a topping of crumbled feta cheese and breadcrumbs.

2 LARGE AUBERGINES

2 TABLESPOONS OLIVE OIL

1 LARGE ONION, FINELY CHOPPED

2-3 CLOVES OF GARLIC, CRUSHED

1 RED PEPPER, CORED, DESEEDED AND CHOPPED

500 G (1 LB) EXTRA LARGE SUN-RIPENED TOMATOES, SKINNED,

DESEEDED AND CHOPPED

2 TABLESPOONS CHOPPED PARSLEY

PINCH OF SUGAR (OPTIONAL)

SALT AND PEPPER

CHOPPED PARSLEY TO GARNISH

Cut the aubergines in half lengthways and scoop out most of the filling, leaving a thin wall. Chop the aubergine flesh, put in a colander, sprinkle with salt and leave for 30-60 minutes. Sprinkle salt inside the aubergine shells and leave upside down for 30-60 minutes. Rinse the aubergine shells and flesh, and dry well.

Heat the oil in a pan, add the onion and garlic and cook, stirring occasionally, until softened. Stir in the aubergine flesh and red pepper, cook for 2-3 minutes, then stir in the tomatoes, parsley and seasoning. Bring to the boil and simmer for about 15 minutes, stirring occasionally, until lightly thickened. Adjust the seasoning and add a pinch of sugar if necessary.

Place the aubergine shells, skin side down, in a sauté pan, deep frying pan or lightly oiled shallow baking dish. Divide the filling between the shells and pour 2-3 tablespoons water around them to cover the base of the pan or dish. Cover and cook gently on top of the hob, or in a preheated oven, 200°C (400°F), Gas Mark 6, for about 30 minutes until the aubergines are tender, and the cooking juices have evaporated. Sprinkle with parsley and allow to cool a little before eating.

Serves 4

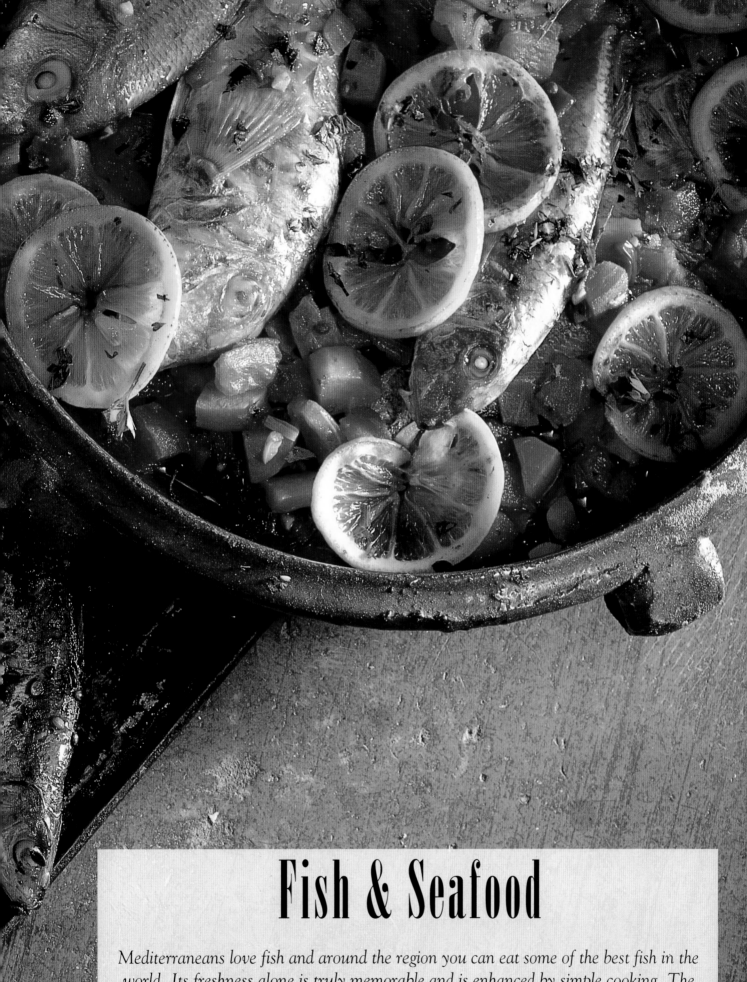

Fish & Seafood

Mediterraneans love fish and around the region you can eat some of the best fish in the world. Its freshness alone is truly memorable and is enhanced by simple cooking. The most popular method is grilling, preferably over an open fire, with fresh herbs or spices added, and a sharp-tasting ingredient, such as lemon or lime juice, tomatoes, capers or olives, to highlight the wonderful flavour of the fish.

RED MULLET IN VINE LEAVES

There is a dichotomy of opinion as to whether the scales of barbecued red mullet should be left on. If they are, they coalesce in the fierce heat of the fire to form a protective crust that keeps the flesh moist and tender; also the sea salt they contain will be concentrated, intensifying the tangy, sea-fresh flavour. The skin must, of course, then be removed before the fish is eaten. Others prefer to scale the fish before cooking to allow the flesh to be impregnated by the delicious flavour of the fire. It is often said that red mullet should be cooked like woodcock, with the liver still in situ to impart a gamey flavour to the flesh, but most red mullet on sale nowadays (which has probably been frozen even if sold 'fresh') is pre-gutted.

2 LARGE, SUN-RIPENED TOMATOES, SKINNED, DESEEDED AND CHOPPED

2 CLOVES OF GARLIC, FINELY CRUSHED

4 ANCHOVY FILLETS, CHOPPED

4 TABLESPOONS CHOPPED PARSLEY

2 TABLESPOONS CHOPPED BASIL

12 VINE LEAVES

4 RED MULLET, EACH WEIGHING ABOUT 250 G (8 OZ), SCALED AND RINSED

OLIVE OIL FOR BRUSHING

SALT AND PEPPER

TO GARNISH (OPTIONAL)

ANCHOVY FILLETS

BLACK OLIVES

Mix the tomatoes, garlic, anchovy fillets, parsley, basil and black pepper together with a fork.

Arrange 3 vine leaves slightly overlapping so they will fit under one fish. Spread one quarter of the tomato mixture over the leaf in the centre, then place one fish on the leaves. Fold the leaves over the fish to form a parcel. Repeat with the remaining leaves, fish and tomato mixture.

Place the parcels in a single layer in a baking tin, brush with oil and bake in a preheated oven, 200°C (400°F), Gas Mark 6, for 15 minutes. Carefully transfer to a warm serving plate and garnish with anchovy fillets and olives, if liked.
Serves 4

Overleaf:
From left to right: Red Mullet in Vine Leaves,
Tunisian Grilled Sardines and Fish Plaki

TUNISIAN GRILLED SARDINES WITH TOMATO RELISH

With one of the richest and most diverse catches of fish in the Mediterranean, Tunisia has some delicious fish dishes.

16 FRESH SARDINES

SPRIGS OF CORIANDER TO GARNISH (OPTIONAL)

MARINADE

1 CLOVE OF GARLIC

2 TEASPOONS CORIANDER SEEDS, TOASTED

1 DRIED RED CHILLI, DESEEDED AND CHOPPED

FINELY GRATED RIND AND JUICE OF 1 LIME

4 TABLESPOONS VIRGIN OLIVE OIL

SALT AND PEPPER

RELISH

4 SPRING ONIONS, WHITE PART ONLY, CHOPPED

JUICE OF 1 LIME

250 G (8 OZ) SUN-RIPENED TOMATOES, SKINNED, DESEEDED AND CHOPPED

1 HALF OF SUN-DRIED TOMATO, CHOPPED

½ DRIED RED CHILLI, DESEEDED AND CHOPPED

3 TABLESPOONS CHOPPED CORIANDER

Using the back of a knife, de-scale the sardines. Cut off the fins with scissors and cut along the stomach. Remove and discard the intestines. Wash the fish thoroughly, pat dry with kitchen paper and lay in a shallow, non-metallic dish.

Using a pestle and mortar, pound the garlic, coriander seeds and chilli together with a pinch of salt. Add the lime rind and juice, gradually work in the oil. Pour over the sardines, coat well with the mixture, cover and leave for about 1 hour, turning 2 or 3 times.

Blend the relish ingredients in a processor or blender. Cook the sardines under a grill for 2-3 minutes each side, basting with marinade. Serve with the relish, and garnish with coriander if liked.
Serves 4

Variation
Sardines with Lemon and Parsley – mix together 6 tablespoons olive oil, 3 tablespoons lemon juice, 2 tablespoons chopped parsley and salt and pepper. Brush the mixture over 1 kg (2 lb) prepared fresh sardines. Marinate for 1 hour, then cook fish under a preheated grill for 2-3 minutes each side, brushing with the lemon mixture as the fish browns and when turning it. Serve with the remaining lemon mixture poured over, and lemon wedges.

FISH PLAKI

Plakis are a feature of both Turkish and Greek cuisines, but typically in Turkey the fish is cut into steaks or pieces and it may be served cold, whereas the fish in a Greek plaki is cooked whole. Lemon is also characteristic of the Greek version.

APPROXIMATELY 1.25 KG (2½ LB) FISH SUCH AS BREAM, STRIPED BASS,
GREY MULLET, RED SNAPPER OR POMPANO, CLEANED AND SCALED

1 LARGE LEMON

2 TABLESPOONS VIRGIN OLIVE OIL

1 ONION, CHOPPED

1 CARROT, FINELY CHOPPED

2 CLOVES OF GARLIC, CHOPPED

1 TEASPOON CORIANDER SEEDS, CRUSHED

500 G (1 LB) RIPE TOMATOES, SKINNED, DESEEDED AND CHOPPED

3 HALVES OF SUN-DRIED TOMATO, CHOPPED

75 ML (3 FL OZ) MEDIUM-BODIED DRY WHITE WINE

LEAVES FROM A BUNCH OF PARSLEY, FINELY CHOPPED

SALT AND PEPPER

Put the fish into a baking dish. Squeeze the juice from half the lemon and pour over the fish.

Heat the olive oil in a saucepan, add the onion and carrot and cook, stirring occasionally, until the onion has softened but not coloured. Stir in the chopped garlic and cook for about 3 minutes.

Stir in the coriander seeds, tomatoes, sun-dried tomatoes, wine, parsley and salt and pepper and simmer for a few minutes until well blended. Using a fish slice, lift the fish and pour about a quarter of the tomato mixture underneath. Lay the fish down again. Pour over the remaining tomato mixture. Thinly slice the remaining lemon half and lay the slices on top of the fish.

Cover the dish and bake in a preheated oven, 190°C (375°F), Gas Mark 5, for about 40 minutes until the fish flakes when tested with the point of a sharp knife.

Serves 4

Variation
Cook sliced celery and/or sliced fennel with the onion and omit the coriander seeds.

SKATE WITH CAPER AND ANCHOVY SAUCE

Wild capers cling to apparently inhospitable rocky cracks and stone walls and in the Mediterranean in May, harvesters will have to comb the countryside gathering the buds as they burst into beautiful white or pink flowers with flowing purple stamens. Since caper bushes are usually scattered, pickers have to walk about a kilometre (over ½ mile) to collect 1 kg (2 lb) of buds. Even harvesting from cultivated bushes is back-breaking work. Although the vast majority of capers are preserved in vinegar, a few are packed in salt and these are well-worth snapping up if you see them; simply rinse off the salt before using. Spain is the world's largest producer of capers, with the majority grown in Andalusia, the Balearics and Murcia, where I tasted the most successful pairing of capers and local salted anchovies in a piquant sauce that really bought the skate to life.

1 CLOVE OF GARLIC, CRUSHED

4 ANCHOVY FILLETS, RINSED IF NECESSARY

1¼ TEASPOONS MUSTARD

1½ TABLESPOONS CAPERS, RINSED

2 TABLESPOONS CHOPPED PARSLEY

1 TABLESPOON CHOPPED TARRAGON

2 TABLESPOONS VIRGIN OLIVE OIL

4 TABLESPOONS LIME JUICE

2 TABLESPOONS OLIVE OIL

2 SKATE WINGS

SALT AND PEPPER

Crush the garlic with a pinch of salt using a pestle and mortar. Work in the anchovy fillets to make a paste, then mix in the mustard, capers, herbs, virgin olive oil, lime juice and pepper.

Heat the olive oil in a wide frying pan. Season the skate, using very little salt, add to the pan and fry over a high heat for 4-5 minutes each side, depending on the thickness.

Add the sauce and heat briefly to warm through.

Serves 2

TUNA WITH SUN-DRIED TOMATOES, OLIVES AND SAGE

Tuna fisheries have existed in the Mediterranean for centuries and have been of major commercial importance, but now they are declining, along with a reduction in the size of the catch. Sicily is one place where there are still a number and the tuna trap, the 'tonnare', is a much-enjoyed ritual. This recipe is based on a dish served to me in Sicily by the cousin of an Italian friend. It has the typical impact of a southern dish, but unusually includes sage rather than chilli.

350 ML (12 FL OZ) MEDIUM-BODIED DRY WHITE WINE

350 ML (12 FL OZ) FISH STOCK

10 OIL-CURED BLACK OLIVES, PITTED AND SOAKED
IN WARM WATER FOR 10 MINUTES

4 TABLESPOONS OLIVE OIL

4 FRESH TUNA STEAKS, ABOUT 200 G (7 OZ) EACH

1 SMALL ONION, FINELY CHOPPED

50 G (2 OZ) SUN-DRIED TOMATOES PACKED IN OIL,
DRAINED AND CUT INTO STRIPS

2 TEASPOONS FINELY CHOPPED SAGE

SQUEEZE OF LEMON JUICE

PEPPER

SAGE LEAVES TO GARNISH (OPTIONAL)

Boil the wine in a wide frying pan until reduced by half, then add the stock and boil until reduced to 250 ml (8 fl oz). Meanwhile, drain and chop the olives.

Heat the oil in a heavy frying pan, add the tuna and cook until browned on both sides, but still pink in the centre, about 4-5 minutes each side. Transfer to a warm plate, cover and keep warm. Add the onion to the frying pan and cook, stirring, for about 2 minutes. Stir in the reduced wine and stock, the tomatoes and chopped sage and bring to the boil, scraping the bottom of the pan to dislodge the sediment. Boil until the liquid is reduced to 175 ml (6 fl oz). Add the olives and lemon juice and pepper to taste. Pour over the fish and serve garnished with sage leaves, if liked.

Serves 4

SQUID WITH PEPPERS AND LEMON

This recipe from Pescara shows the characteristic Calabrian predilection for dishes packed with punchy flavour. Use small squid that are fresh and not frozen; check when buying the squid, as fish and seafood in display cabinets that looks fresh is often thawed frozen fish. To prepare fresh squid, follow the instructions in Calabrian Stuffed Squid (see page 69).

500 G (1 LB) CLEANED SQUID

3 TABLESPOONS OLIVE OIL

1 RED PEPPER, CORED, DESEEDED AND CHOPPED

2 CLOVES OF GARLIC, CHOPPED

1 DRIED RED CHILLI, CRUMBLED

FINELY GRATED RIND OF 1 SMALL LEMON

3 TABLESPOONS LEMON JUICE

1 TABLESPOON CHOPPED PARSLEY

SALT AND PEPPER

TO SERVE

LEMON WEDGES

COUNTRY BREAD (SEE PAGE 113)

Chop the squid tentacles roughly, and cut the bodies into 5-10 mm (¼-½ inch) thick rings.

Heat the oil in a sauté pan or deep frying pan, add the red pepper, garlic, chilli and lemon rind and cook fairly gently, stirring occasionally, for about 5 minutes. Increase the heat to moderately high, stir in the squid and sauté until it becomes opaque and just tender, about 1-1½ minutes. Transfer to a warmed serving dish, sprinkle over salt, pepper and lemon juice to taste, sprinkle with parsley and serve immediately with lemon wedges and Country Bread.

Serves 4

*Left: Tuna with Sun-dried
Tomatoes, Olives and Sage
Right: Squid with Peppers and Lemon*

BREAM IN COUSCOUS JACKET, WITH TOMATO AND MINT SALAD

Several varieties of sea-bream are found in the Mediterranean – dentex, bogue, gilthead (daurade) and black-banded, with the best eating usually considered to be the dentex and gilthead. Fortunately, both are becoming more readily available here. The crisp, nutty coating in this recipe keeps the breams' flesh beautifully succulent and traps in the flavour.

I PLUMP CLOVE OF GARLIC, CRUSHED

I TEASPOON LIME JUICE

I TEASPOON WHITE WINE VINEGAR

5 TABLESPOONS OLIVE OIL

2 LARGE SUN-RIPENED TOMATOES, SKINNED, DESEEDED AND CHOPPED

25 G (I OZ) MINT, CHOPPED

40 G (I½ OZ) FINE COUSCOUS

20 G (¾ OZ) BLANCHED ALMONDS, FINELY CHOPPED

I SPRING ONION, THINLY SLICED

4 SEA-BREAM EACH WEIGHING ABOUT 250 G (8 OZ), CLEANED AND SCALED

I EGG, SIZE 2, BEATEN

SALT AND PEPPER

Stir together the garlic, lime juice, vinegar and half the olive oil. Season then pour over the tomatoes, add half the mint and gently toss together. Cover and refrigerate.

Mix together the couscous, almonds, spring onion, the remaining mint, plenty of black pepper and a little salt.

Dip each fish in the egg, then coat evenly with the couscous mixture.

Heat the remaining olive oil in a large, preferably non-stick, frying pan. Add the fish in a single layer and fry for about 7 minutes each side until the flesh flakes when tested with the point of a knife. Serve immediately with the tomato and mint salad.

Serves 4

BAKED FISH WITH 'HOT' TAHINI SAUCE

Baking fish under a coating of flavoured tahini is a favourite Lebanese method. The rich sauce bastes and flavours the fish and keeps the flesh moist and succulent.

I SNAPPER OR OTHER BAKING FISH, WEIGHING ABOUT 2 KG (4 LB), CLEANED AND SCALED, HEAD AND TAIL LEFT ON

4-6 CLOVES OF GARLIC

4 TABLESPOONS FINELY CHOPPED CORIANDER

100 ML (3½ FL OZ) OLIVE OIL

125 ML (4 FL OZ) LEMON JUICE

125 ML (4 FL OZ) WATER

250 ML (8 FL OZ) TAHINI

¼-½ TEASPOON HOT CHILLI POWDER

I TABLESPOON TOASTED PINE NUTS

SALT

TO GARNISH

LEMON WEDGES

CORIANDER SPRIGS

With the point of a sharp knife, cut 2 or 3 slashes in each side of the fish, then rub the fish, inside and out, with salt. Cover and refrigerate for 1-2 hours.

Meanwhile, pound the garlic with a pinch of salt then mix in the coriander.

Wipe the fish dry. Heat the oil in a large frying pan, add the fish and cook over a high heat for about 3 minutes each side. Transfer the fish to a baking dish and sprinkle with 1½ tablespoons of the lemon juice.

Pour all but 2 tablespoons of the oil from the pan. Stir in the garlic mixture and fry quickly until crisp, but do not allow it to burn. Remove from the heat.

Gradually beat the water into the tahini – the mixture will thicken. Next, gradually beat in the remaining lemon juice, then stir in the garlic mixture and chilli powder to taste.

Pour over the fish, covering it completely and bake in a preheated oven, 180°C (350°F), Gas Mark 4, for about 30-35 minutes until the fish is cooked through and the sauce is bubbling. Scatter the pine nuts over the fish and serve garnished with lemon wedges and coriander sprigs.

Serves 4

CALABRIAN STUFFED SQUID

The Calabrian coastline meanders its way around the 'boot' of Italy for 180 kilometres (the longest of Italy's regions), with small craggy bays and deep water on the west contrasting with shallow waters and longer beaches on the east. Yet, surprisingly, fishing does not play a very large part in local life. Squid, however, is popular.

I KG (2 LB) SMALL WHOLE SQUID

2 TABLESPOONS OLIVE OIL

75 G (3 OZ) SPRING ONIONS, WHITE PART ONLY, FINELY CHOPPED

3 CLOVES OF GARLIC, CRUSHED

175-200 G (6-7 OZ) DRAINED, COOKED SPINACH

2 TABLESPOONS CHOPPED PARSLEY

SALT AND PEPPER

To prepare the squid, hold the head just below the eyes, gently pull it away from the body and discard the soft innards that come away with it. Pull out and discard the fine, flexible quill that is attached to the inside of the body pouch. Cut the head from the tentacles just below the eyes and discard. The tentacles are joined together – in the centre is a beak-like mouth, which can be removed by squeezing it out. Slip your fingers under the skin covering the body and peel it off. Cut the fins away from either side of the pouch. Rinse the pouch and dry thoroughly. Chop the tentacles.

Heat I tablespoon of the oil in a frying pan, add the spring onions and garlic and cook, stirring occasionally, for 2-3 minutes. Stir in the chopped tentacles, cook for a further 2-3 minutes, then tip into a food processor or blender. Add the spinach and seasoning and process for about 1½ minutes.

Divide the spinach mixture between the body pouches of the squid, close the openings with wooden cocktail sticks and place the squid close together in a single layer in a shallow baking dish. Sprinkle over the remaining oil and bake in a preheated oven, 180°C (350°F), Gas Mark 4, for about 20 minutes, until the squid are tender.

Remove the cocktail sticks and sprinkle with the parsley.

Serves 4

BAKED STUFFED SARDINES

Dishes of stuffed sardines are popular in Italy, particularly throughout the south. The stuffing is usually placed between two flattened sardines, like a sandwich, which may either be baked, or coated in egg and breadcrumbs and deep-fried. A little grated Pecorino Romano can be added to this stuffing and sprinkled on the fish with the breadcrumbs. Serve 1 'sandwich' per person for an antipasto, 2 for a main course

12 FRESH SARDINES

I CLOVE OF GARLIC

I TABLESPOON EACH CHOPPED PARSLEY, CHIVES, DILL AND ROSEMARY

2 SMALL SAGE LEAVES, CHOPPED

25 G (I OZ) PINE NUTS, LIGHTLY TOASTED AND COARSELY CHOPPED

2 TABLESPOONS LIGHT VIRGIN OLIVE OIL

½ LEMON

SCANT 15 G (½ OZ) FRESH BREADCRUMBS

SALT AND PEPPER

Cut the heads and tails from the sardines and slit along the underside of the bodies to open them out. Discard the intestines. Wash the cavities of the fish and pat dry with kitchen paper. Lay one fish, skin-side uppermost, on a work surface and press gently along the centre of the back with your thumbs to dislodge the backbone. Turn the fish over and gently pull away the backbone. Repeat with the remaining sardines.

Chop the garlic and herbs together finely, then mix with the pine nuts, I tablespoon of the oil and seasoning.

Oil a wide shallow baking dish with a little of the remaining oil and lay 6 of the sardines, skin-side down, in a single layer in it. Squeeze over some lemon juice, then spread some of the herb mixture on each fish. Cover with the remaining sardines, skin-side up. Sprinkle with the breadcrumbs then trickle over the remaining oil. Bake in a preheated oven, 220°C (425°F), Gas Mark 7, for about 10 minutes, until golden. Serve hot or at room temperature.

Serves 3

PRAWNS WITH FETA

If you are in Tourkalimenos in Piraeus, you will find this dish in all the restaurants. It may either be baked in an earthenware dish so the cheese is lightly browned or cooked on top of the stove. Traditionally, the prawn shells are left on, which means eating them is not the easiest of things, so if you prefer, remove the body shells before cooking, leaving just the heads and tails in place.

3 TABLESPOONS OLIVE OIL

I ONION, FINELY CHOPPED

2 CLOVES OF GARLIC, CRUSHED

4 OR 5 LARGE SUN-RIPENED TOMATOES, SKINNED, DESEEDED AND CHOPPED

3 TABLESPOONS CHOPPED PARSLEY

2 TEASPOONS DRIED OREGANO

75 ML (3 FL OZ) MEDIUM-BODIED DRY WHITE WINE (OPTIONAL)

I KG (2 LB) RAW LARGE PRAWNS, IN THEIR SHELLS

75-125 G (3-4 OZ) EWES' MILK FETA CHEESE

PEPPER

COARSELY CHOPPED PARSLEY TO GARNISH

Heat the oil in a flameproof earthenware casserole, add the onion and garlic and fry, stirring occasionally, until softened but not coloured. Stir in the tomatoes, parsley, oregano and wine, if using and simmer until reduced and lightly thickened. Season with pepper (the cheese will add salt).

Gently stir the prawns into the sauce and simmer for 4-5 minutes. Crumble over the feta cheese and cook for a further 5 minutes. Serve garnished with the coarsely chopped parsley.

If cooking in the oven, bake in a preheated oven, 180°C (350°F), Gas Mark 4, for 15 minutes.

Serves 4

GOLDEN ESCABECHE

In the days before refrigeration and deep-freezing, when there was too much fish to be eaten immediately, it would be cooked, then steeped in an acid-based marinade to help extend its edible life and so save many a case of food poisoning; spices or herbs were often included to make dull fish more interesting. The name 'escabèche' is derived from the Perso-Arabic word 'sikbaj', which means 'vinegar stew', and similar dishes for meat, poultry, game and vegetables, as well as fish, are found along the length of the Mediterranean shores.

6-8 FILLETS OF SEA BREAM, SCALED WITH THE SKIN LEFT ON

3 TABLESPOONS SEASONED WHITE FLOUR

3 TABLESPOONS VIRGIN OLIVE OIL

MARINADE

2 TABLESPOONS VIRGIN OLIVE OIL

2 RED ONIONS, THINLY SLICED

1½ TEASPOONS CUMIN SEEDS, LIGHTLY CRUSHED

½ TEASPOON DRIED RED CHILLI FLAKES

2 RED PEPPERS, CORED, DESEEDED AND SLICED

LARGE PINCH OF SAFFRON STRANDS, CRUSHED AND SOAKED

IN 3 TABLESPOONS WATER

FINELY SHREDDED RIND AND JUICE OF I ORANGE

2-3 TABLESPOONS LEMON JUICE

CASTER SUGAR TO TASTE

SALT AND PEPPER

CHOPPED CORIANDER OR PARSLEY TO GARNISH

For the marinade, heat the oil, add the onions and cook for 2 minutes. Stir in the cumin seeds and chilli flakes for about 45 seconds. Add the peppers and fry, stirring occasionally, until soft, then add the saffron and liquid, orange rind and juice and lemon juice. Bubble for a few minutes and add sugar and seasoning to taste. Leave to cool.

Coat the fish in the seasoned flour, then fry in the oil until browned and just cooked through, about 2-3 minutes each side. Using a fish slice, transfer the fish to a shallow non-metallic dish, leave to cool, then pour over the cooled marinade. Cover, place in the refrigerator and leave fish for 4-12 hours, turning carefully 2 or 3 times. Return to room temperature 30 minutes before serving garnished with coriander or parsley.

Serves 4 as a main course, 6-8 as a first course

Clockwise from top: Prawns with Feta,
Golden Escabeche and
Turkish Skewered Swordfish

TURKISH SKEWERED SWORDFISH

Traditionally, the best place to eat fish in Turkey is Istanbul and some of the best I've eaten there has been bought from the most unpretentious of places – the flotilla of boats bobbing at the Eminonu end of the Galata Bridge. Here, arms reach up from the boats offering strollers enticing packages and fragrant skewers which have been cooked over braziers and charcoal burners wedged precariously in the little craft.

625 G (1¼ LB) SWORDFISH, CUT INTO APPROXIMATELY

2.5 × 4 CM (1 × 1½ INCH) CUBES

OIL FOR GREASING

LEMON WEDGES TO SERVE (OPTIONAL)

MARINADE

4 TABLESPOONS LEMON JUICE

4 TABLESPOONS OLIVE OIL

3 TABLESPOONS FINELY CHOPPED RED ONION

2 BAY LEAVES, TORN

1½ TEASPOONS PAPRIKA

SALT AND PEPPER

LEMON SAUCE

3 TABLESPOONS VIRGIN OLIVE OIL

3 TABLESPOONS LEMON JUICE

3 TABLESPOONS CHOPPED PARSLEY

SALT AND PEPPER

Mix together the marinade ingredients. Lay the cubes of swordfish in a single layer in a wide, shallow, non-metallic dish. Pour over the marinade, turn the swordfish so it is evenly coated, cover and leave in a cool place for 4-5 hours, turning the fish occasionally.

Mix together the lemon sauce ingredients and set aside. Oil a grill rack.

Thread the fish on to 4 skewers and cook under a preheated grill or over a hot barbecue for 4-5 minutes each side, basting frequently with the marinade. Serve with the lemon sauce and lemon wedges, if liked.

Serves 4

FISH TAGINE WITH CHERMOULA

Chermoula is the name given to a popular characterful Moroccan marinade that is frequently used with many different types of fish which are to be baked, fried or grilled. However, don't expect fish with chermoula always to taste more or less the same because almost every cook has their own version – parsley may take the place of coriander, onion is sometimes added, chilli may be more or less pronounced and the ratio of other spices will fluctuate.

750 G (1½LB) GREY MULLET, BREAM OR MONKFISH FILLETS

3 TABLESPOONS OLIVE OIL

3 CLOVES OF GARLIC, CRUSHED

1½ TEASPOONS GROUND CUMIN

1 TEASPOON PAPRIKA

1 FRESH GREEN CHILLI, FINELY CHOPPED

HANDFUL OF CORIANDER LEAVES, FINELY CHOPPED

4 TABLESPOONS LEMON JUICE

SALT

LEMON WEDGES TO SERVE

Place the fish fillets in a shallow non-metallic dish. Mix together the olive oil, garlic, ground cumin, paprika, green chilli, chopped coriander, lemon juice and salt and pour over the fish. Cover and leave in a cool place for 3-4 hours, turning occasionally.

Cook the fish fillets under a preheated grill for about 4 minutes each side, basting with the coriander mixture occasionally, until the flesh flakes when tested with the point of a sharp knife. Serve warm with lemon wedges.

Serves 4

MOROCCAN PRAWNS WITH SPICES

Whenever I cook this dish my mind flies back to a glorious evening, when I was sitting beneath a deep royal blue Tangier sky, the sleepy sounds of night drawing in and the exotic aroma of prawns being cooked in this way wafting tantalizingly past my nose. The prawns can also be butterflied (use scissors to cut the prawns lengthways almost in half, leaving the tails intact), then marinated in the spice mixture before grilling for 3-4 minutes; brush with any remaining marinade during cooking.

500 G (1 LB) RAW KING PRAWNS IN THEIR SHELLS

4 TABLESPOONS OLIVE OIL

2 CLOVES OF GARLIC, CRUSHED

1 TEASPOON GROUND CUMIN

½ TEASPOON GROUND GINGER

1 TEASPOON PAPRIKA

¼ TEASPOON CAYENNE PEPPER

LEAVES FROM A BUNCH OF CORIANDER, FINELY CHOPPED

SALT

LEMON WEDGES TO SERVE

Remove the shells, legs, heads and tails from the prawns. Cut along the back with the point of a sharp knife and remove the dark thread.

Heat the olive oil in a frying pan, add the garlic and cook until it becomes aromatic. Stir in the cumin, ginger, paprika and cayenne pepper, heat for about 30 seconds, then add the prawns. Fry quickly, stirring, until they turn pink. Stir in the coriander, heat for about 30 seconds, then serve the prawns with the cooking juices spooned over and accompanied by lemon wedges.

Serves 4

GRILLED BUTTERFLIED PRAWNS WITH ROMESCO SAUCE

Gambas and langostini are large prawns suitable for this recipe. Nora peppers are sold by specialist Spanish food shops, but if unavailable use 1 large red pepper, charred, skinned and deseeded, and 1-2 small dried red chillies, soaked for 20 minutes in cold water and drained.

12-16 RAW JUMBO PRAWNS IN THEIR SHELLS

3 TABLESPOONS OLIVE OIL

½ CLOVE OF GARLIC, FINELY CRUSHED

1½ TABLESPOONS LIME JUICE

SALT AND PEPPER

LEMON WEDGES TO SERVE

SAUCE

2 NORA PEPPERS, DESEEDED, SOAKED FOR 20 MINUTES IN COLD WATER, DRAINED (SEE ABOVE)

4 PLUMP CLOVES OF GARLIC, GRILLED AND SKINNED

150 G (5 OZ) MIXED HAZELNUTS AND BLANCHED ALMONDS, TOASTED

SMALL HANDFUL OF PARSLEY

4 TABLESPOONS RED WINE VINEGAR

150 ML (¼ PINT) OLIVE OIL

To make the sauce, pound the peppers, garlic, nuts, parsley and seasoning to a paste in a mortar or mix in a food processor or blender. Mix in the vinegar, then slowly pour in the oil; the mixture should be thick and almost smooth. Adjust the seasoning and add a little more vinegar if necessary. Transfer to a bowl, cover and refrigerate for at least 1 day, or up to 1 week; transfer to room temperature 2 hours before serving.

Remove the legs and heads from the prawns. Using sharp scissors, cut each prawn lengthways from the head end almost to the tail; leave the tail intact. Place in a shallow dish. Mix together the remaining ingredients, pour over the prawns, turn to coat with the marinade, leave for 30 minutes.

Cook under a preheated grill, brushing occasionally with any remaining marinade, until the prawns have opened out (butterflied) and are bright pink, about 3 minutes. Just before the prawns are ready, stir the sauce then serve with the prawns, accompanied by lemon wedges.

Serves 4

Variation
Omit the parsley; reduce the almonds to 25 g (1 oz) or use 25 g (1 oz) browned hazelnuts and add 250 g (8 oz) extra large tomatoes, charred, skinned and deseeded.

Meat & Poultry

Around the Mediterranean meat is at a premium, so it is highly respected and cooked in the most sympathetic and quality-enhancing ways – often 'stretched' by the addition of pulses, rice, pasta, fruit and vegetables. Climate and religion dictate that lamb is the most common type of meat. Chickens are kept by many households, and game is enormously popular – hunting is a favourite pastime for the men of the region – and a rabbit hutch or pigeoncote housing unsuspecting occupants is still a common sight.

CHICKEN TAGINE WITH OLIVES AND PRESERVED LEMONS

This is one of the best-known Moroccan dishes. It cannot be made with fresh lemons, or, if it is, it will be an entirely different dish. Lemons preserved in salt lose their sharpness and have a mellow flavour which is complemented by pinky-brown Moroccan olives. If you are unable to find Moroccan olives, substitute Greek Kalamatas.

2 TABLESPOONS OLIVE OIL

I SPANISH ONION, FINELY CHOPPED

3 CLOVES OF GARLIC

I TEASPOON GROUND GINGER

I½ TEASPOONS GROUND CINNAMON

LARGE PINCH OF SAFFRON THREADS, TOASTED AND CRUSHED

I CHICKEN WEIGHING ABOUT 1.75 KG (3½ LB)

750 ML (1¼ PINTS) CHICKEN STOCK OR WATER

125 G (4 OZ) GREENY-BROWN MOROCCAN OLIVES,
RINSED, AND SOAKED IF LIKED

I PRESERVED LEMON (SEE NOTE OPPOSITE), RINSED IF LIKED, CHOPPED

LARGE BUNCH OF CORIANDER, FINELY CHOPPED

LARGE BUNCH OF PARSLEY, FINELY CHOPPED

SALT AND PEPPER

COARSELY CHOPPED PARSLEY TO GARNISH

Heat the oil, add the onion and fry fairly gently, stirring frequently, until softened and a good golden colour.

Meanwhile, in a mortar, crush the garlic with a pinch of salt, then work in the ginger, cinnamon, saffron and a little pepper. Stir into the onions, cook until fragrant, then remove from the pan and spread over the chicken. Put the chicken in a heavy saucepan or flameproof casserole that it just fits, add the stock or water and bring to just on simmering point. Cover and simmer very gently for about 1¼ hours, turning the chicken over 2 or 3 times.

Add remaining ingredients to the pan, cover again and cook for a further 15 minutes or so until the chicken is very tender. Taste the sauce – if the flavour needs to be more concentrated, transfer the chicken to a warm shallow serving dish, cover and keep warm, then boil the cooking juices to a rich sauce. Tilt the pan and skim off surplus fat, if liked, then pour over the chicken and garnish with parsley.

Serves 4

Overleaf:
Clockwise from top right: Chicken Tagine
with Olives and Preserved Lemons,
Arni Frikase and Pork with Fennel

Note
Preserving Lemons

To preserve lemons, put 2 teaspoons of coarse salt in a scalded Kilner or parfait jar. Holding a lemon over a plate to catch the juice and using a sharp, stainless steel knife, cut lengthways as if about to quarter it, but do not cut quite through – leave the pieces joined. Ease out any pips.

Pack I tablespoon of salt into the cuts, then close them and place in the jar. Repeat with more lemons, packing them tightly and pressing each layer down hard before adding the next layer, until the jar is full. Squeeze another lemon and pour the juice over the fruit. Sprinkle with more coarse salt and top up with boiling water to cover the lemons.

Close the jar tightly and keep in a warmish place for 3-4 weeks. Do not worry if, on longer storage, a lacy white film appears on top of the jar or on the lemons; it is quite harmless – simply rinse it off.

If liked, a mixture of I stick of cinnamon, 3 cloves, 6 crushed coriander seeds, 3 black peppercorns and I bay leaf can be layered with the lemons.

ARNI FRIKASE

*Arni Frikase is simply a lamb casserole and may be
flavoured with one or more of a number of vegetables, such
as carrots, celery, lettuce, peas, artichokes and celeriac.
This version reminds me of a lunch I enjoyed on the island
of Cos, when a similar recipe was served for everyone
seated around the rough wooden tables outside the taverna.
The only accompaniments were home-made bread to mop up
the juices and wine to wash down the fragrant meal.*

625 G (1¼ LB) BONED SHOULDER OF LAMB, CUBED

I ONION, THINLY SLICED

I CARROT, THINLY SLICED

I STICK OF CELERY, THINLY SLICED

BOUQUET GARNI INCLUDING OREGANO, SAVORY AND THYME

4-6 ARTICHOKES, TRIMMED (SEE PAGE 54)

125 G (4 OZ) BABY ONIONS, PEELED, OR LARGE SPRING ONION BULBS

I TIGHT COS LETTUCE, QUARTERED LENGTHWAYS

4 EGG YOLKS, SIZE 2

3-4 TABLESPOONS LEMON JUICE

SALT AND PEPPER

CHOPPED DILL TO SERVE

Put the lamb, onion, carrot, celery, bouquet garni and
seasoning in a heavy, flameproof casserole and add water to
cover. Heat to just on simmering point, remove the scum
from the surface, cover the casserole and cook very gently
for about 30 minutes. Add the artichokes and baby onions, if
used, and cook for a further 35 minutes or so, until the
meat and artichokes are just about tender. If using spring
onion bulbs, add them 5 minutes before the end. Add the
lettuce and cook for a further 5 minutes.

Using a slotted spoon, transfer the meat and vegetables to
a warm serving dish, cover and keep warm. Discard the
bouquet garni.

Tilt the casserole, spoon off the fat from the surface of
the cooking liquid, then boil the liquid, if necessary, to make
about 300 ml (½ pint).

Stir the egg yolks with the lemon juice and dill, stir in a
ladleful of the cooking liquid, then pour back into the
casserole and heat gently, stirring, until lightly thickened.
Lightly but thoroughly stir into the meat and vegetables.
Serves 4

PORK WITH FENNEL

*The lift and faint sweetness that the aniseed flavour of
fennel gives to pork is further highlighted by the last minute
addition of gremolada, an Italian mixture of finely grated
lemon rind and finely chopped parsley and garlic.*

APPROXIMATELY I KG (2 LB) LEAN PORK, CUT INTO LARGE CHUNKS

I TEASPOON CHOPPED THYME

I TEASPOON FENNEL SEEDS, CRUSHED

2 CLOVES OF GARLIC, CHOPPED

450 ML (¾ PINT) MEDIUM-BODIED DRY WHITE WINE

SEASONED PLAIN FLOUR

3 TABLESPOONS EXTRA VIRGIN OLIVE OIL

125 G (4 OZ) PIECE OF PANCETTA, CUT INTO THIN STRIPS

2 ONIONS, SLICED

2 FENNEL BULBS

SALT AND PEPPER

GREMOLADA

I½ TEASPOONS FINELY GRATED LEMON RIND

½ CLOVE OF GARLIC, FINELY CHOPPED

2 TABLESPOONS CHOPPED PARSLEY

FEATHERY FENNEL FRONDS, CHOPPED (SEE METHOD)

Put the pork into a non-metallic dish, sprinkle over the
thyme, fennel seeds and garlic, then pour over the wine.
Cover and leave to marinate in a cool place for 4-12 hours,
turning the pork occasionally.

Lift the pork from the marinade, pat dry and coat lightly
with seasoned flour. Heat I tablespoon of the oil in a heavy
flameproof casserole, add the pancetta and cook until lightly
browned and the fat runs. Transfer to kitchen paper. Add
the pork to the casserole in batches and brown evenly.
Transfer to kitchen paper to drain.

Add remaining oil and onions to pan, fry gently 5-8 minutes
until soft and beginning to brown. Pour in marinade, stirring
to dislodge the sediment, and bring to the boil. Bubble for a
couple of minutes, then return the pork and pancetta to the
pan. Season, cover tightly and cook gently on the hob or in a
preheated oven, 160°C (325°F), Gas Mark 3, for I hour.

Trim and reserve the feathery fronds from the fennel
bulbs, then cut each bulb into six wedges. Add to the
casserole, cover again and cook for a further 30 minutes
until the pork and fennel are tender. Mix together the
gremolada ingredients and scatter over the casserole.
Serves 5-6

CHICKEN À LA PROVENCALE

Fragrant smells redolent of a Provençal food market or busy kitchen creep enticingly from the oven while the chicken is cooking, waiting to explode in an aromatic cloud of tomato, anchovy, olives and herbs when the lid is lifted.

10 CLOVES OF GARLIC

1 TABLESPOON FINELY CHOPPED THYME

1 TABLESPOON FINELY CHOPPED MARJORAM

1.75 KG (3½ LB) CHICKEN, SKINNED AND QUARTERED

4 TABLESPOONS LEMON JUICE

4 TABLESPOONS OLIVE OIL

1 SPRIG OF THYME

SMALL SPRIG OF ROSEMARY

6 BASIL LEAVES, TORN

8 ANCHOVY FILLETS, SOAKED IF NECESSARY, CHOPPED

4 LARGE WELL-FLAVOURED TOMATOES, SKINNED, DESEEDED AND CHOPPED

150 ML (¼ PINT) MEDIUM-BODIED DRY WHITE WINE

24 NICOISE OLIVES

SALT AND PEPPER

CHOPPED MIXED PROVENCAL HERBS, SUCH AS BASIL, THYME, MARJORAM AND ROSEMARY, TO GARNISH

Crush 2 cloves of garlic with a small pinch of salt and the chopped herbs, either in a mortar using a pestle, or a small bowl using the end of a rolling pin, or using the flat of the blade on a chopping board. With the point of a sharp knife, make cuts in the chicken and insert some of the garlic and herb mixture in each cut. Rub with lemon juice and pepper, cover and leave in a cool place for 2 hours.

Heat 2 tablespoons of the oil in a saucepan. Chop the remaining garlic and add it and the thyme, rosemary and basil. Cook over a moderate heat, stirring occasionally, for about 5 minutes. Stir in the anchovy fillets, tomatoes and wine and simmer for about 15 minutes. Add pepper to taste (salt will be unnecessary because of the saltiness of the anchovies and olives).

Heat the remaining oil in a heavy, flameproof casserole, add the chicken and brown evenly; cook the chicken in batches if necessary to avoid crowding. Add the olives to the sauce, pour over the chicken, cover tightly and cook in a preheated oven, 160°C (325°F), Gas Mark 3, for 45 minutes, turning the chicken once or twice. Add the olives and cook for a further 15 minutes or so until the chicken is tender. Discard the herb sprigs. Serve with Provençal herbs sprinkled over.

Serves 4

RABBIT WITH CORIANDER, SAFFRON AND ALMONDS

Spain has had a thriving rabbit population for at least 2,000 years. There is a theory that the old name for Spain, Hispania, is derived from a Phoenician word variously spelt as 'i-sephamin' or 'i-saphan-im', meaning 'island or coast of rabbits'. This Andalusian-inspired rabbit dish, heady with the flavours of rich olive oil, garlic, saffron and coriander features a typical Spanish way of thickening sauces using crushed fried bread, garlic and almonds.

6-8 CLOVES OF GARLIC

75 G (3 OZ) BLANCHED ALMONDS

4-5 TABLESPOONS VIRGIN OLIVE OIL

2 SLICES OF FRENCH BREAD, EACH ABOUT 1 CM (½ INCH) THICK

1 TEASPOON CUMIN SEEDS

1 BUNCH OF CORIANDER, CHOPPED

LARGE PINCH OF SAFFRON STRANDS, TOASTED AND CRUSHED

3 TABLESPOONS MEDIUM-BODIED DRY WHITE WINE, WARMED

4 GOOD SIZE RABBIT PORTIONS

2-3 TABLESPOONS LEMON JUICE

SALT AND PEPPER

CORIANDER SPRIGS TO GARNISH

LEMON WEDGES TO SERVE

Fry the garlic and almonds in 1 tablespoon of the oil in a fairly small frying pan until lightly browned. Using a slotted spoon, transfer to kitchen paper to drain. Add a further 2 tablespoons of the oil to the pan, add the bread and fry until golden and crisp on both sides. Transfer to kitchen paper. Stir the cumin seeds into the pan and heat for 1-2 minutes until fragrant. Scoop out on to the garlic and almonds, then add the coriander to the pan and stir until wilted. Put all the fried ingredients into a mortar, add the saffron and pound with a pestle, or use the end of a rolling pin in a bowl. Then mix in the wine to make a smooth paste.

Heat the remaining oil in a heavy flameproof casserole, add the rabbit portions and brown lightly. Pour over the saffron paste and sufficient water to come about halfway up the rabbit, add seasoning, cover the casserole tightly and cook very gently for about 45 minutes, turning the rabbit over halfway through, until it is tender. Add the lemon juice and cook, uncovered, for a further 5 minutes. Transfer the rabbit to a warmed serving plate; if the sauce needs to be reduced further, boil it to the right consistency. Pour over the rabbit, garnish with coriander. Serve with lemon wedges.

Serves 4

CHICKEN WITH RED PEPPERS AND TOMATOES

Fat, juicy peppers are a recurring and endearing feature of the vibrant, cheerful and full, sunny-flavoured Catalan cuisine. Grilling them, preferably over embers, along with other vegetables, is almost in the blood of Catalans. The characteristic depth and smokiness that grilling gives to the peppers adds a complexity and richness to the taste of this casserole, but it is not essential and the step can be omitted if you prefer.

1.5 KG (3 LB) CHICKEN, JOINTED

I TEASPOON PAPRIKA

4 RED PEPPERS

3 TABLESPOONS OLIVE OIL

125 G (4 OZ) SALTED PORK BELLY OR STREAKY BACON, CUT INTO STRIPS

2 ONIONS, THINLY SLICED

3 CLOVES OF GARLIC, CHOPPED

4 LARGE SUN-RIPENED TOMATOES, SKINNED, DESEEDED AND CHOPPED

I BOUQUET GARNI OF 4 SPRIGS OF PARSLEY,

2 SPRIGS OF THYME AND I BAY LEAF

100 ML (3½ FL OZ) MEDIUM-BODIED DRY WHITE WINE

SALT AND PEPPER

CHOPPED PARSLEY TO GARNISH

Season the chicken portions and rub with the paprika. If liked and time permits, grill the peppers until evenly charred and blistered. Leave until cool enough to handle, then remove the skins. Cut the peppers into halves, discard the cores and seeds and slice the flesh.

Heat the oil in a heavy flameproof casserole, add the pork or bacon and brown for about 2 minutes. Remove to a large plate with a slotted spoon. Add the chicken to the casserole and brown evenly. Transfer to the plate.

Stir the onions and garlic into the casserole and cook, stirring occasionally, until softened and translucent. Stir in the tomatoes and bouquet garni and simmer for 15 minutes. Stir in the wine and pepper strips. Bring to the boil, add the chicken and pork or bacon and any juices that have collected on the plate, cover tightly and cook gently for 40-45 minutes until the chicken is tender. Serve sprinkled with chopped parsley.

Serves 4

STIFATHO

We always seem to think of Greece as being a hot country, but during the winter in the mountains it can become cold. Then, warming, sustaining food is called for, such as this lightly spiced, savoury stew. The country peasants did not have access to top-quality beef, so they cooked their beef slowly in red wine and vinegar to tenderize it. This lengthy cooking also gives the dish its special flavour, so it is necessary for a true Greek Stifatho. It is therefore both inappropriate and inadvisable to use a prime cut.

3 TABLESPOONS OLIVE OIL

I KG (2 LB) LEAN CHUCK STEAK, CUT INTO LARGE CUBES

I KG (2 LB) BABY OR PICKLING ONIONS, PEELED

3 CLOVES OF GARLIC, CRUSHED

4 LARGE SUN-RIPENED TOMATOES, SKINNED, DESEEDED AND CHOPPED

2 BAY LEAVES

3-4 CLOVES

I CINNAMON STICK

250 ML (8 FL OZ) RED WINE

3 TABLESPOONS RED WINE VINEGAR

APPROXIMATELY I TEASPOON SUGAR

SALT AND PEPPER

Heat the oil in a frying pan, add the beef in batches so that it is not crowded and cook until evenly browned. Using a slotted spoon, transfer the beef as it is done to a heavy, preferably earthenware, flameproof casserole. Stir the onions into the pan and cook, stirring occasionally, until browned. Stir in the remaining ingredients dislodging the sediment. Bring to the boil, then pour over the meat. Cover tightly with greaseproof paper, then a heavy lid. Cook over a very low heat, using a heat diffusing mat, if necessary, for about 3 hours, stirring occasionally, until the beef is very tender. Alternatively, cook in a preheated oven, 160°C (325°F), Gas Mark 3.

If there is too much liquid towards the end of the cooking time, uncover the casserole. If there is still too much at the end of the cooking time, pour it into a frying pan and boil until reduced. Remove the cinnamon and check the sweetness, adding more sugar or vinegar as necessary. Pour back into the casserole and stir to mix.

Serves 6

MOUSSAKA

Moussaka is an Arabic name given to a Greek pie of minced meat layered with vegetables, usually aubergines, then covered by a white sauce. It derives from 'muhklabah', a medieval Arab dish made of rice and sometimes nuts as well as aubergines and minced meat. It was taken through the streets of country villages to be put in the baker's oven to cook. Moussaka shares a number of features with Baked Lasagne (see page 105) – both are layered and include similar minced meat and béchamel sauces and both are much abused. If you do not have time to leave the milk to infuse, omit the carrot, onion and bay leaf and, instead, flavour the sauce with a little freshly grated nutmeg. The béchamel sauce can be made in advance and left for a couple of hours in a cool place, with a sheet of greaseproof paper lying on the surface, or overnight in the refrigerator. You may need to stir in a little milk before using it, as it will thicken on standing. Moussaka always tastes better if it is made a day in advance and reheated.

3 AUBERGINES, CUT INTO SLICES ABOUT 1 CM (½ INCH) THICK

1 LARGE ONION, FINELY CHOPPED

3 CLOVES OF GARLIC, CRUSHED

OLIVE OIL FOR FRYING

625 G (1¼ LB) LEAN LAMB, MINCED

625 G (1¼ LB) SUN-RIPENED TOMATOES, CHOPPED

2 HALVES OF SUN-DRIED TOMATOES, CHOPPED

1 TEASPOON GROUND CINNAMON

1 TABLESPOON CHOPPED PARSLEY

50 G (2 OZ) KEFALOTIRI OR PARMESAN CHEESE, GRATED

SALT AND PEPPER

BECHAMEL SAUCE

600 ML (1 PINT) MILK

¼ ONION

PIECE OF CARROT

SPRIG OF PARSLEY

1 BAY LEAF

50 G (2 OZ) UNSALTED BUTTER

3 TABLESPOONS PLAIN FLOUR

2 EGGS, BEATEN

SALT AND PEPPER

Sprinkle the aubergine slices generously with salt, put in a colander and leave for 30-60 minutes. Rinse well and dry with kitchen paper.

Meanwhile, fry the chopped onion and crushed garlic in a little olive oil in a large frying pan, until lightly browned. Add the minced lamb and cook until browned, stirring to break up any lumps. Stir in the chopped tomatoes, sun-dried tomatoes, cinnamon, chopped parsley and a little black pepper and simmer gently for about 20 minutes, stirring occasionally, until the sauce is thick.

To make the béchamel sauce, gently heat the milk in a saucepan with the vegetables and herbs, until the milk comes to the boil. Remove from the heat, then cover the pan, leave for 15 minutes, then strain.

Melt the butter in a heavy-bottomed saucepan, gradually stir in the flour and cook for about 30 seconds. Over a low heat, slowly pour in the milk, stirring constantly, then bring to the boil, stirring. Simmer for about 5 minutes, stirring occasionally. Remove from the heat and stir in the beaten eggs and seasoning to taste.

Heat a thin layer of oil in a large frying pan, add the aubergine slices in batches and fry until golden on both sides. Using a slotted spoon, transfer the slices to kitchen paper to drain.

Layer the aubergines and meat mixture in a casserole, ending with a layer of aubergines. Pour over the béchamel sauce, sprinkle evenly with the grated cheese then bake, uncovered, in a preheated oven, 180°C (350°F), Gas Mark 4, for 45 minutes until golden.

Serves 6

CHICKEN BREASTS WITH FRAGRANT HERB STUFFING

*Although fresh herbs are now available all year round,
I prefer to reserve a recipe like this – where their flavour
affects the quality – for summer cooking when the sun will
have given them more taste.*

50 G (2 OZ) MIXED HERBS SUCH AS BASIL, THYME, MARJORAM AND PARSLEY

1 CLOVE OF GARLIC

25 G (1 OZ) SOFT CHEESE, SUCH AS RICOTTA

APPROXIMATELY 5 TABLESPOONS OLIVE OIL, PLUS EXTRA FOR BRUSHING

15 G (½ OZ) PARMESAN CHEESE, FRESHLY GRATED

1 TABLESPOON PINE NUTS, CHOPPED

4 LARGE CHICKEN BREASTS, SKINNED

4 TABLESPOONS MEDIUM-BODIED DRY WHITE WINE

SALT AND PEPPER

Pound the herbs, garlic and a pinch of salt together in a mortar with a pestle or chop finely using a mezzaluna, then transfer to a small bowl. Work in the soft cheese, then the oil. Lastly add the Parmesan cheese, pine nuts and pepper. If time allows, leave for 1-2 hours for the flavours to develop.

Place 1 chicken breast at a time between 2 sheets of clingfilm, flatten slightly using a meat bat or rolling pin, then cut a deep pocket. Lay each breast on a piece of lightly oiled foil. Season lightly, spoon some herb paste into each pocket and seal with wooden cocktail sticks. Fold up the foil and spoon in 1 tablespoon of wine. Fold the foil over the chicken to form loose parcels, securing the edges tightly. Place on a baking sheet and cook in a preheated oven, 180°C (350°F), Gas Mark 4, for 30-40 minutes, until the chicken is tender.

Serve the chicken warm with the cooking juices spooned over or leave to cool in the foil and serve sliced.
Serves 4

Variation
Chicken Breast Rolls with Tapenade – marinate the breasts in lemon juice and thyme for 8 hours. Beat out as above, spread with Tapenade (see page 23), then roll up and wrap in a slice of bacon, enclosing a sprig of thyme on one side and a bay leaf on the other. Cook as above.

PIGEON NICOISE

It is well known that Frenchmen have a penchant for shooting virtually anything that flies, so the pigeons that raid their vineyards, fruit bushes and gardens are certainly classed as fair game. The typically robust Provençal flavours of this recipe will not be lost against the taste of wild birds, and the red wine marinade will coax tough flesh into mellowness. On the other side of the coin, it gives character to young farm-reared birds and makes them taste more of the wild.

4 OVEN-READY YOUNG PIGEONS

2 ONIONS, SLICED

3 CLOVES OF GARLIC, CUT INTO THIN SLIVERS

½ BUNCH PARSLEY

475 ML (16 FL OZ) RED WINE

75 ML (3 FL OZ) BRANDY

6 ANCHOVY FILLETS, SOAKED IF NECESSARY

125 G (4 OZ) PITTED NICOISE OLIVES

50 G (2 OZ) UNSALTED BUTTER

OLIVE OIL FOR BRUSHING

SALT AND PEPPER

PARSLEY LEAVES TO GARNISH

Put the pigeons in a single layer in a non-metallic dish. Scatter the onions, garlic and parsley over and around the birds. Pour over the wine and 50 ml (2 fl oz) of the brandy. Cover and leave for several hours, turning the birds occasionally.

Meanwhile, using a pestle and mortar, pound the anchovy fillets with the remaining brandy, olives and butter. Add plenty of black pepper.

Lift the pigeons from the marinade, pat dry and brush with olive oil. Cook under a preheated grill, basting frequently with the marinade, for 20-30 minutes until the skin is crisp and brown and the flesh still slightly pink. Leave in a warm place for 10-15 minutes, then halve each bird along the backbone and breast bone. Spread each half with the anchovy and olive mixture and serve immediately, garnished with parsley leaves.
Serves 4

SOUVLAKIA

The only time skewers of grilled cubes of lamb used to be found in Greece was during fiestas. Then, village cafés and stalls with 'mangali', portable charcoal braziers, would cook them to order, threading individually specified quantities of lean and fat meat on long metal skewers, 'souvles', cooking them, then placing in a split pitta with a sprinkling of chopped onion and parsley. Now, they are almost ubiquitous throughout Greece.

1 TABLESPOON OREGANO

4 TABLESPOONS OLIVE OIL

2 TABLESPOONS LEMON JUICE

625 G (1¼ LB) BONED LEG OF LAMB, CUT INTO CUBES

SALT AND PEPPER

TO GARNISH (OPTIONAL)

1 SPANISH ONION, QUARTERED THEN THINLY SLICED

LEMON WEDGES

Crush the oregano in a mortar with a pestle or in a bowl using the end of a rolling pin, then mix in the oil, lemon juice and pepper.

Thread the lamb on to small skewers. Lay the skewers in a shallow dish and pour over the oil mixture. Turn the skewers so the lamb is evenly coated and leave in a cool place for 1-1½ hours.

Grill the lamb skewers under a preheated grill or over a barbecue fire, turning frequently, until the lamb is brown on the outside but still just pink inside, about 5-10 minutes. Sprinkle with salt and garnish with sliced onion and lemon wedges, if liked.

Serves 4

LAMB AND OKRA STEW

Middle Eastern dishes using okra are often simply called 'bamia', the ethnic name for okra, no matter what the other ingredients. Small pods of okra are preferred and it is important when trimming off the conical cap not to pierce the inner seed pod, so allowing the sticky liquid it contains to seep out. Bamia without meat is often served hot or cold as a main course on fast days, but it also makes a good accompaniment to grilled or roasted meats or poultry.

3 TABLESPOONS VEGETABLE OIL

1 KG (2 LB) LEAN LAMB, CUBED

1 LARGE ONION, CHOPPED

3 CLOVES OF GARLIC

1 TEASPOON GROUND CORIANDER

½ TEASPOON GROUND CUMIN

500 G (1 LB) OKRA, TRIMMED

4 SUN-RIPENED TOMATOES, SKINNED, DESEEDED AND CHOPPED

1-2 TABLESPOONS TOMATO PUREE

LEMON JUICE TO TASTE

SALT AND PEPPER

PARSLEY OR CORIANDER TO GARNISH

Heat the oil in a heavy flameproof casserole, add the lamb in batches and cook until brown. Using a slotted spoon, transfer the lamb to a bowl. Stir the onion and garlic into the casserole and cook, stirring occasionally, until lightly browned. Stir in the ground coriander and cumin, then add the okra. Cook for a few minutes more, stir in the tomatoes and tomato purée and enough lemon juice to taste; cook for a further 2-3 minutes.

Return the lamb to the casserole with any juices that have collected in the bowl. Add the seasonings and sufficient water almost to cover the lamb and bring to just simmering point. Cover tightly and cook gently for about 1½ hours until the lamb is very tender; gently stir occasionally during cooking and add a little warm water if necessary, but at the end of cooking the sauce should be thick. Serve sprinkled with parsley or coriander.

Serves 4-6

Left: Souvlakia
Right: Lamb and Okra Stew

CHICKEN CASSEROLE WITH ALMONDS

Body is given to this lightly spiced Moroccan sauce by the finely chopped onion and almonds that are added at the beginning of the cooking so that they soften during the long, slow cooking.

1 LEMON, HALVED

4 CHICKEN QUARTERS

½ TEASPOON GROUND GINGER

½ TEASPOON GROUND CINNAMON

PINCH OF SAFFRON THREADS, TOASTED AND CRUSHED

1 SPANISH ONION, FINELY CHOPPED

125 G (4 OZ) BLANCHED ALMONDS, CHOPPED

LEAVES FROM A LARGE BUNCH OF PARSLEY, FINELY CHOPPED

SALT AND PEPPER

Squeeze the lemon over the chicken, rub in the juice and season with salt and pepper. Mix together the ginger, cinnamon and saffron and spread over the chicken. Leave at room temperature for about 1 hour. Put the portions into a heavy flameproof casserole in which they just fit. Add the onion and almonds and sufficient water almost to cover.

Bring to just on simmering point, cover and simmer very gently for about 45-60 minutes, turning the chicken occasionally. Add the parsley and cook for a further 5 minutes.

Transfer the chicken to a warm plate, cover and keep warm. Boil the cooking juices to give a well-flavoured sauce, adjusting the levels of the spices and seasonings, if necessary. Return the chicken to the casserole and turn in the sauce to coat.

Serves 4

AFELIA WITH PORK

Afelia is a Cypriot style of cooking vegetables or pork with coriander seeds and red wine and all dishes cooked in this way, irrespective of the main ingredient, are called simply 'afelia'. Cypriots are so fond of the taste of coriander seeds that the fragrant berries are a hallmark of the island's cooking. Adjust the level of coriander seeds according to your own taste.

750 G (1½ LB) LEAN BONELESS SHOULDER OF PORK, CUBED

200 ML (7 FL OZ) FULL-BODIED RED WINE, OR MORE IF LIKED

1-2 TABLESPOONS CRUSHED CORIANDER SEEDS

4 TABLESPOONS OLIVE OIL

SALT AND PEPPER

FRESH CORIANDER SPRIGS TO GARNISH

Put the pork in an earthenware dish, pour over the wine and sprinkle with the coriander seeds and black pepper. Stir well, cover and leave in a cool place for 8-12 hours, turning the meat over occasionally.

Using a slotted spoon, remove the pork from the dish and dry on kitchen paper. Reserve the wine.

Heat the oil in a flameproof casserole, add the pork and fry, stirring occasionally, until evenly browned. Add the reserved wine and salt, bring to just below simmering point, cover tightly and cook very gently, stirring occasionally, for about 1 hour until the pork is very tender. Serve garnished with coriander sprigs.

Serves 4

POT ROAST CHICKEN WITH LEMON AND ROSEMARY

When I ate this fairly standard Italian family chicken dish at the home of some friends near Amalfi, I was quite taken aback by the wonderful fragrant intensity of the lemon flavour. The local lemons were responsible, so I brought home a couple of dozen. I am now pleased to find that they are being imported into this country – they are larger than other lemons we get and have a fruitier fragrance.

2 TABLESPOONS OLIVE OIL

15 G (½ OZ) UNSALTED BUTTER

I CHICKEN WEIGHING ABOUT 1.75 KG (3½ LB), JOINTED

2 CLOVES OF GARLIC, FINELY CRUSHED

125 ML (4 FL OZ) MEDIUM-BODIED DRY WHITE WINE

I SPRIG OF ROSEMARY

2 TABLESPOONS LEMON JUICE

PIECE OF LEMON RIND CUT INTO 5-6 FINE STRIPS

SALT AND PEPPER

Heat the oil and butter in a heavy, flameproof casserole. Add the chicken, skin-side down, and brown quickly and lightly, adding the garlic towards the end.

Stir in the wine, add the rosemary and seasoning, bubble for 2-3 minutes, then lower the heat, cover tightly and cook very gently for about 45-50 minutes, turning the chicken a couple of times, until the juices run clear.

Transfer the chicken to a warm serving plate, cover and keep warm in the oven with the heat turned off. Discard the rosemary then tilt the casserole and skim off most of the fat. Stir in the lemon juice to dislodge the sediment, add the strips of rind and bring to the boil over a high heat, stirring. Pour over the chicken.

Serves 4

STUFFED WHOLE COURGETTES

4 COURGETTES, ABOUT 175 G (6 OZ) EACH

I TABLESPOON OLIVE OIL

250 G (8 OZ) LEAN MINCED LAMB

½ TEASPOON GROUND ALLSPICE

I ONION, FINELY CHOPPED

I CLOVE OF GARLIC, CHOPPED

I TEASPOON CRUMBLED DRIED MINT

2 TABLESPOONS PINE NUTS, LIGHTLY TOASTED

250 ML (8 FL OZ) GREEK EWES' MILK YOGURT

I TABLESPOON SESAME SEEDS, LIGHTLY TOASTED, TO GARNISH

Cut off and reserve the stem ends of the courgettes. Using an apple corer, hollow out the courgettes, taking care not to pierce the skins and leaving 5 mm (¼ inch) thick shells. Chop the scooped out flesh and reserve.

Heat the oil in a frying pan over a fairly high heat until hot but not smoking, add the minced lamb and allspice and cook, stirring, until the lamb is no longer pink. Using a slotted spoon, transfer to a sieve to drain. Pour off all but I tablespoon of fat from the pan. Add the onion to the pan and cook, stirring occasionally, until softened. Add the garlic and reserved courgette flesh and cook, stirring occasionally, until pale golden. Stir in the cooked lamb, mint, pine nuts, 2 tablespoons yogurt and salt and pepper. Leave to cool.

Divide the meat mixture between the courgette shells, replace the ends and secure with wooden cocktail sticks. Place in a steaming basket over a saucepan of simmering water, cover and steam for 20-25 minutes, until tender.

Meanwhile, warm the remaining yogurt to serve with the courgettes. The courgettes can either be served whole accompanied by the warm Greek yogurt sprinkled with sesame seeds, or cut into 2.5 cm (I inch) thick slices, arranged on a large warm serving plate or individual plates, sprinkled with sesame seeds and a spoonful of yogurt added.

Serves 4

Variation

Stuffed Courgette Boats – trim the ends from 4 medium-large courgettes, then halve lengthways. Using a teaspoon or melon baller, scrape out and discard all the seeds. Steam the courgette halves for about 5 minutes, or until slightly relaxed. Arrange them as upright as possible in an oiled grill pan. Mash together 250 g (8 oz) ewes' milk feta cheese, 2 beaten eggs, approximately 1½ tablespoons dill and season with pepper – no salt is required because of the saltiness of the cheese. Spoon into the courgettes and grill until well browned. Serve warm.

CIRCASSIAN CHICKEN

This classic Turkish recipe dates from the time of the Ottoman Empire in Turkey, when Circassian women captives in the Sultans' harems were renowned for their beauty and their culinary skills. The dish is garnished in characteristically Turkish fashion with walnut oil flavoured with paprika. It is traditionally served lukewarm as a first course, but is also good cold, or hot if the chicken is reheated in the sauce. Unless all the nuts are absolutely fresh, cook another recipe instead.

1 CHICKEN, WEIGHING ABOUT 1.75 KG (3½ LB)

1 ONION, QUARTERED

1 CARROT, QUARTERED

1 BOUQUET GARNI

175 G (6 OZ) SHELLED FRESH WALNUTS

50 G (2 OZ) CRUSTLESS COUNTRY BREAD (SEE PAGE 113)

1 CLOVE OF GARLIC, CRUSHED

2 TABLESPOONS WALNUT OIL

1 TEASPOON PAPRIKA

SALT AND PEPPER

CHOPPED PARSLEY TO GARNISH

Put the chicken into a saucepan in which it just fits, tuck the onion, carrot and bouquet garni around the bird, season and pour in sufficient water to come about two thirds of the way up the chicken. Bring to just boiling point, remove any scum, then cover and simmer very gently for about 1¼ hours, until the chicken is tender. Remove the chicken from the pan and leave until cool enough to handle. Boil the stock in the saucepan to reduce. Remove the skin and bones from the chicken and add them to the pan; slice the chicken flesh into neat portions and set aside.

Meanwhile, grind the fresh nuts with the bread in a blender. Add the garlic, then gradually add sufficient of the strained stock (about 250 ml (8 fl oz)) to give a light creamy sauce. Mix half of the sauce with the chicken, pile on to a serving plate, then pour over the remaining sauce. Leave until lukewarm.

Just before serving mix the walnut oil with the paprika and trickle over the chicken. Garnish with a sprinkling of chopped parsley.

Serves 6 as a first course, 4 as a main course

KLEFTIKO

The name of this Cypriot dish originates from sheep rustlers who used to cook their meat in a sealed earthenware thick casserole, a 'tava', buried in a fire so that the fragrant smells of the cooking would not waft into the air and give them away. To seal the lid, make a thick flour and water paste, roll it into a sausage and wrap around the join. Serve with plenty of lemon; a crisp green salad makes a good accompaniment.

1 SHOULDER OF LAMB, CUT INTO 4-6 PIECES OR 4-6 PIECES OF SHOULDER, WITH A TOTAL WEIGHT OF ABOUT 375 G (12 OZ), WELL TRIMMED

1 LARGE ONION, FINELY CHOPPED

2-3 CLOVES OF GARLIC, CHOPPED

4-5 TABLESPOONS LEMON JUICE

SEVERAL SPRIGS OF OREGANO

1 LARGE SPRIG OF ROSEMARY

2 BAY LEAVES

3 TABLESPOONS OLIVE OIL

SALT AND PEPPER

PLENTY OF LEMON WEDGES TO SERVE

Put the meat into a heavy, preferably earthenware, casserole then add the onion, garlic, lemon juice, herbs, oil, salt and pepper and sufficient water to come halfway up the lamb. Seal the lid in place with a flour and water paste and bake in a preheated oven, 160°C (325°F), Gas Mark 3, for at least 2½ hours without removing the lid.

If possible, leave the meat to cool in the cooking liquid for several hours, preferably overnight, then gently but thoroughly heat through again the next day. Alternatively, check to see if the lamb is tender. When it is, pour off and reserve the cooking liquid and cook the meat, uncovered, at 200°C (400°F), Gas Mark 6, until lightly browned, about 20 minutes. Serve with lemon wedges.
Serves 6

GRILLED CHICKEN WITH CUCUMBER, YOGURT AND MINT SALAD

Around the Mediterranean, the preferred way to grill foods is in the centuries-old manner – over an open fire – as it gives a most appetizing flavour to the food. At an open-air party I was lucky enough to attend in the foothills of the Rif mountains, the flavour of grilled spices added another layer to the taste sensations. These in turn, were beautifully offset by the cool mixture of cucumber, yogurt and mint that appears throughout southern and eastern Mediterranean countries and is variously referred to as a sauce, salad or relish. In Turkey, it goes under the name of 'cacik', in Greece 'tzatziki'.
The sauce can be omitted and the cooked chicken sprinkled with chopped coriander.

4 CHICKEN PORTIONS

5 TABLESPOONS OLIVE OIL

2 CLOVES OF GARLIC, FINELY CRUSHED

1¼ TABLESPOONS PAPRIKA

1¼-1½ TEASPOONS GROUND CUMIN

SQUEEZE OF LEMON JUICE

PINCH OF CAYENNE PEPPER

SALT

SAUCE

½ CUCUMBER, PEELED AND HALVED LENGTHWAYS

175 ML (6 FL OZ) GREEK EWES' MILK YOGURT

1 CLOVE OF GARLIC, CRUSHED

1-1½ TABLESPOONS CHOPPED MINT

SALT AND PEPPER

Put the chicken in a wide shallow dish. Mix together the oil, garlic, paprika, cumin, lemon juice and cayenne, pour over the chicken, turn to coat, then cover and leave in a cool place for 2 hours, turning the chicken 2 or 3 times.

Meanwhile, make the sauce. Scoop out and discard the seeds from the cucumber. Chop the cucumber, sprinkle with salt and leave in a colander for 30-60 minutes to drain. Rinse the cucumber and dry well with kitchen paper. Mix together the yogurt, garlic, mint and pepper, then stir in the chopped cucumber, pour into a serving bowl, cover and leave in the refrigerator.

Sprinkle salt over the skin side of the chicken and place under a preheated grill for 8-10 minutes, until the skin is golden, brushing with the oil mixture remaining in the dish.

Turn the chicken over, sprinkle with salt and brush with the cooking juices and remaining oil mixture. Cook for a further 10 minutes or so until the juices run clear when the thigh is pierced with a sharp knife. Serve with the cucumber sauce.
Serves 4

Variation

Grilled Chicken with Herb and Lemon Marinade – place 4 chicken breasts in a single layer in a shallow non-metallic baking dish. Mix together the grated rind and juice of 1 lemon, 1 tablespoon olive oil, the finely chopped white and 2.5 cm (1 inch) green part of 2 spring onions, 1 tablespoon chopped fresh thyme, 1½ tablespoons chopped coriander, ¼ teaspoon ground coriander, salt and pepper. Pour over the chicken, cover and refrigerate for 8 hours, turning occasionally. Grill as above, basting occasionally. Serve garnished with coriander sprigs.

CHICKEN WITH SAGE AND LEMON

A title this simple is not the sort to lead a prospective diner to expect anything out of the ordinary. But how wrong I was when I ordered this in Florence. The dish that arrived was a perfect example of how simplicity can be delicious.

4 CHICKEN BREASTS, SKINNED

5 TABLESPOONS VIRGIN OLIVE OIL

3 TABLESPOONS LEMON JUICE

28 SMALL SAGE LEAVES

40 G (1½ OZ) UNSALTED BUTTER

SALT AND PEPPER

2 LEMONS, HALVED, TO SERVE

Place the chicken breasts in a single layer in a non-metallic dish. Pour over 3 tablespoons of the oil and the lemon juice. Scatter over the sage leaves, turn the chicken so that the breasts are evenly coated, then cover and leave for about 30 minutes.

Lift the chicken breasts from the marinade and pat dry. Strain the marinade into a small bowl; reserve the sage leaves separately.

Heat the butter and remaining oil in a frying pan, add the chicken, smooth side down, and cook for about 5 minutes, until browned. Turn the chicken breasts, season them and tuck the sage leaves around them. Cook for another 5 minutes or so until the underside is brown and the chicken cooked through.

Transfer the chicken to a warmed serving plate, place the sage leaves on the chicken, cover and keep warm.

Tilt the pan and pour off the fat. Place the pan over the heat and stir in the reserved marinade, dislodging the sediment. Boil until reduced to a brown glaze, then pour over the chicken. Serve with the lemon halves.

Serves 4

Variation

Chicken with Sage and Ham – brown 4 chicken joints in butter and oil in a large frying pan. Add 50 g (2 oz) chopped prosciutto, heat for 1 minute, stir in 300 ml (½ pint) medium-bodied dry white wine, bubble for 1 minute, then lower the heat. Add 1 tablespoon small sage leaves and seasoning, cover and simmer very gently for about 45 minutes. Transfer the chicken to a warmed plate, cover and keep warm. Boil the cooking juices, scraping up the sediment, until lightly thickened. Add a squeeze of lemon juice, then pour over the chicken.

COUSCOUS

This is a favourite North African dish, ideal for an informal meal.

500 G (1 LB) LEAN LAMB, CUT INTO LARGE CUBES

2 ONIONS, QUARTERED THEN THICKLY SLICED

2 CLOVES OF GARLIC, CRUSHED

PINCH OF SAFFRON THREADS, CRUSHED

1 TEASPOON GROUND CINNAMON

½ TEASPOON PAPRIKA

1 FRESH RED CHILLI, DESEEDED AND FINELY CHOPPED

½ TEASPOON GROUND GINGER

250 G (8 OZ) SMALL CARROTS, QUARTERED LENGTHWAYS

250 G (8 OZ) SMALL TURNIPS, QUARTERED

250 G (8 OZ) KOHLRABI OR CELERIAC, CUT INTO LARGE CHUNKS

500 G (1 LB) PRE-COOKED COUSCOUS

2 TEASPOONS OLIVE OIL

250 G (8 OZ) COURGETTES, QUARTERED LENGTHWAYS

250 G (8 OZ) BROAD BEANS

4 TOMATOES, QUARTERED

LARGE BUNCH EACH PARSLEY AND CORIANDER, CHOPPED

40 G (1½ OZ) UNSALTED BUTTER

SALT AND PEPPER

Put the lamb in a large saucepan. Add 900 ml (1½ pints) water, the onion, garlic, spices and seasoning. Bring to the boil, remove the scum from the top, cover and simmer very gently for about 30 minutes. Add the carrots, turnips and kohlrabi or celeriac, cover again and simmer for 15 minutes.

Put the couscous into a large bowl, pour over about 300 ml (½ pint) water, stir well and leave for 10 minutes. Add another 300 ml (½ pint) water and the oil and fork through the couscous to make sure the grains are separate, then leave for 10 minutes until swollen and tender but still separate. Put into a steamer and place, uncovered, over a saucepan of boiling water for about 10 minutes.

Meanwhile, add the courgettes and broad beans to the lamb. Add the tomatoes and herbs and cook for a further 5 minutes until the vegetables and lamb are tender.

Fork through couscous to separate the grains, then turn on to a large serving plate. Dot the butter over the top, stir in and season. Form into a mound with a large well in the centre, place lamb in the well. Using a slotted spoon, lift the vegetables from the cooking broth and place on and around the lamb. Serve remaining broth in a separate warm bowl.

Serves 4

PIGEON WITH KUMQUATS

In countries where red meat is limited, pigeons are a welcome addition to the diet, and so pigeoncotes are a common rural and urban sight in the Middle East. The birds are small and tender, more like Western farm-reared pigeons than wild ones. In addition, every year, hundreds of thousands of birds pass over the Mediterranean on their journeys to and from their summer and winter haunts. Each time, many hapless birds, especially quail and pigeons, fall victim to the hunters' guns – to end up in the cooking pot. If kumquats are not available, add 2 peeled and thickly sliced oranges when the cooking liquid is almost reduced.

3 TABLESPOONS OLIVE OIL

6 YOUNG OVEN-READY PIGEONS

250 G (8 OZ) BUTTON ONIONS, PEELED

I CINNAMON STICK

I BAY LEAF

¾-I TEASPOON GRATED FRESH ROOT GINGER

LARGE PINCH OF SAFFRON THREADS, TOASTED AND CRUSHED

900 ML (I½ PINTS) CHICKEN STOCK

250 G (8 OZ) KUMQUATS, HALVED

2 TABLESPOONS CLEAR HONEY

SALT AND PEPPER

LIGHTLY TOASTED ALMOND HALVES TO GARNISH

Heat the oil in a large, heavy flameproof casserole, add the pigeons in batches and cook until browned. Using a slotted spoon, transfer to a dish. Stir the onions into the casserole and sauté until golden. Stir in the cinnamon, bay leaf, ginger, saffron, stock and salt and pepper and bring to the boil.

Return the pigeons to the casserole with any juices that have collected in the dish, cover and cook gently, turning the pigeons occasionally, for about I hour, depending on their age, until becoming tender. Add the kumquats and honey, cover again and cook for a further 30-45 minutes until the pigeons are very tender. Using a slotted spoon, transfer the pigeons to a large warmed serving plate, cover and keep warm.

Boil the cooking liquid until lightly thickened. Discard the cinnamon and bay leaf, if liked. Pour the liquid over the pigeons and scatter over the almonds.

Serves 6

LAMB WITH ARTICHOKES

Lamb teamed with artichokes is a dish characteristic of southern Italian cooking. It combines vegetables with meat to make it go further; artichokes grow there in abundance and lamb is the meat most often eaten in a region where meat does not usually form part of the daily diet.

3 TABLESPOONS OLIVE OIL

625 G (I¼ LB) YOUNG LAMB, CUT INTO 2.5 CM (I INCH) CUBES

50 G (2 OZ) PROSCIUTTO, CUT INTO STRIPS

I BUNCH OF SPRING ONIONS, WHITE PART ONLY, CHOPPED

4 ARTICHOKES, TRIMMED (SEE PAGE 54)

175 ML (6 FL OZ) VEAL STOCK

SALT AND PEPPER

CHOPPED MINT TO GARNISH

Heat the oil in a heavy-bottomed flameproof casserole, add the lamb and cook until evenly browned. Transfer to a warm bowl and keep warm. Stir the prosciutto and spring onions into the casserole. Fry for about 30 seconds, then stir in the artichokes. Cook, stirring, for 5 minutes. Stir in the stock and return the lamb to the pan. Cook gently for about 15 minutes until the lamb and artichokes are tender. Add the seasoning and sprinkle with chopped mint.

Serves 4

Variation

Substitute artichokes that have been preserved in oil, adding them about 5 minutes before the lamb is ready, so they heat through; the oil from the artichokes can be used instead of olive oil for frying.

LAMB AND DRIED APRICOT TAGINE

'Tagine' is the Moroccan name both for a casserole or stew and the shallow earthenware pot in which it is cooked. Meat and fruit, fresh or dried, are frequent partners in southern Mediterranean dishes. Moroccans have a sweet tooth and add honey, sugar or both to their tagines. However, I have not done so for this recipe as I think the dried apricots provide sufficient sweetness to give a well-balanced taste.

3-4 TABLESPOONS OLIVE OIL

625 G (1¼ LB) LEAN LAMB, CUBED

1 SPANISH ONION, FINELY CHOPPED

3 CLOVES OF GARLIC, CHOPPED

50 G (2 OZ) FRESH ROOT GINGER, PEELED AND FINELY CHOPPED

2 STICKS OF CELERY, THINLY SLICED

PINCH OF SAFFRON THREADS, TOASTED AND CRUSHED

1 TEASPOON CORIANDER SEEDS, TOASTED AND CRUSHED

1 TEASPOON CUMIN SEEDS, TOASTED AND CRUSHED

150 G (5 OZ) DRIED APRICOTS, SOAKED OVERNIGHT JUST COVERED BY WATER

JUICE OF 1 ORANGE

SALT AND PEPPER

PARSLEY TO GARNISH

Heat the oil in a heavy flameproof casserole, add the lamb and cook until evenly browned. Transfer to a bowl. Stir the onion into the casserole and cook over a fairly low heat, stirring occasionally, until soft and the onion is beginning to colour. Stir in the garlic and ginger, increase the heat to moderate and cook for about 1 minute. Stir in the celery, saffron, coriander and cumin for 30 seconds, then return the lamb and any juices that have collected in the bowl to the casserole. Add salt and pepper and sufficient water just to cover the meat, cover the casserole tightly and cook gently for about 1 hour, stirring occasionally.

Stir the apricots and their soaking liquid, and the orange juice into the lamb, cover again and cook for a further 30 minutes or so until all the ingredients are tender and the liquid is reduced and well flavoured. If there is too much liquid or it is too thin, transfer the meat and vegetables to a warmed serving dish and boil the liquid to concentrate it. Pour into the serving dish and stir the ingredients together. Garnish with parsley.

Serves 4

DAUBE PROVENCAL

The south of France does not always bask in sun. Wintertime in the Provençal and Languedoc hills can be decidedly chilly, calling for a large, slowly simmering pot of wine-laced daube. This daube oozes with the region's flavours – herbs, olives and anchovies. The characteristic flavour and texture result from cooking in a plump earthenware daubière nestled in the fire (see page 11). A daube is much better if it is prepared a day in advance so the flavours can mingle and mellow. The meat can also be marinated in the wine with the herbs if you like. Serve with noodles and a crisp green salad.

250 G (8 OZ) LEAN SALT PORK, OR PIECE OF STREAKY BACON, DICED

1.25 KG (2½ LB) LEAN CHUCK STEAK, CUT INTO 5 CM (2 INCH) CUBES

1 LARGE ONION, CHOPPED

3 CLOVES OF GARLIC, CRUSHED

3 CARROTS, FINELY CHOPPED

3 TOMATOES, CHOPPED

SPRIG EACH OF THYME, MARJORAM, ROSEMARY AND PARSLEY

2 BAY LEAVES

STRIP OF SUN OR OVEN-DRIED ORANGE RIND

2 ANCHOVY FILLETS, SOAKED IF NECESSARY, CHOPPED

6 BLACK PEPPERCORNS, CRUSHED

600 ML (1 PINT) RED WINE

12 NICOISE OLIVES

SALT (OPTIONAL)

Gently cook the pork or bacon in a heavy frying pan until the fat runs. Add the beef in batches and fry, stirring frequently, until browned. Using a slotted spoon, transfer the meat when cooked to a heavy flameproof casserole.

Stir the onion into the frying pan and cook, stirring frequently, until softened and browned. Stir in the garlic towards the end. Stir in the carrots, tomatoes, herbs, orange rind, anchovies, peppercorns and wine to dislodge the sediment. Bring to the boil, pour over the meat, cover tightly and cook in a preheated oven, 160°C (325°F), Gas Mark 3, for about 3½ hours until the meat is meltingly tender. Add the olives 10 minutes before serving. If there is too much liquid or it is too thin, remove the meat and keep warm and boil the cooking liquid to concentrate it. Stir the meat back into the casserole and add salt, if necessary.

Serves 6

Top: Lamb and Dried Apricot Tagine
Bottom: Daube Provençal

POACHED CHICKEN WITH LEMON SAUCE

It seems that every Greek garden, at least out in the country, has a lemon tree because Greeks love the flavour of lemon. It is present in innumerable dishes and is one of the pair of ingredients (the other is egg yolk) that comprise the classic Greek sauce thickener; the sauces themselves then being called Avgolemono (see page 17). In this recipe, the light, sharp lemony sauce poured over delicate, moist chicken makes a delicious and fresh-tasting dish.

3 LEMONS

1 CHICKEN WEIGHING APPROXIMATELY 1.75 KG (3½ LB), JOINTED

3 TABLESPOONS OLIVE OIL

APPROXIMATELY 900 ML (1½ PINTS) CHICKEN STOCK

3 EGG YOLKS, SIZE 2

150 ML (¼ PINT) SOURED CREAM

SALT AND PEPPER

Cut one of the lemons in half and rub over the chicken. If there is time, leave at room temperature for about 1 hour.

Fry the chicken portions in the oil until browned, then transfer to a heavy, wide, flameproof casserole. Pour over sufficient stock just to cover the chicken. Add salt and pepper, bring to just simmering point, cover tightly and poach for 35-45 minutes until the chicken is very tender. Remove the chicken from the dish. Increase the heat beneath the casserole and boil the stock until reduced to about 300 ml (½ pint).

Meanwhile, skin the chicken and remove the flesh from the bones in large pieces. Add skin and bones to the stock and place chicken on a warm dish. Cover and keep warm.

Squeeze the remaining lemons. Blend the egg yolks with 5 tablespoons of lemon juice, then stir in the soured cream. Discard the skin and bones from the stock, then tilt the casserole and skim any fat from the surface. Lower the heat. Stir a few spoonfuls of the stock into the egg yolk mixture, then pour into the casserole. Cook, stirring, until lightly thickened, but do not allow to boil. Adjust the level of lemon juice and seasonings, if necessary. Pour some over the chicken and serve the rest separately in a warmed jug.

To serve cold, place the cooked chicken as it is removed from the bones on a cold plate and leave to cool. Allow the sauce to cool, stirring frequently, then spoon over the chicken pieces.
Serves 4

VEAL WITH SAGE AND PROSCIUTTO

Although nearly every Italian restaurant has several veal dishes on the menu, historically, veal was not used south of Tuscany, with the exception of the Roman speciality, Saltimbocca (see below). Using the same ingredients as Saltimbocca – veal, prosciutto, sage – this recipe is based on one I ate at Arancio d'Oro, a small trattoria in Rome.

15 G (½ OZ) UNSALTED BUTTER

2 TABLESPOONS OLIVE OIL

4 LARGE VEAL CHOPS

175 ML (6 FL OZ) MEDIUM-BODIED DRY WHITE WINE

10 SMALL-MEDIUM SAGE LEAVES, COARSELY CHOPPED

2 SLICES OF PROSCIUTTO, FINELY CHOPPED

VEAL STOCK OR WATER (OPTIONAL)

PEPPER

LEMON WEDGES TO SERVE

Heat the butter and oil in a large, heavy frying pan over a moderate heat. Add the veal and cook until golden brown on both sides, about 5 minutes. Add the wine, bubble gently until almost evaporated, then add the sage and prosciutto. Lower the heat and cook gently for about 10 minutes, turning the veal once, until cooked through. Stir in stock or water, if necessary to prevent the veal becoming dry. Season with pepper then transfer the veal to a serving plate. Stir the juices to dislodge the sediment, adding stock or water if necessary, then pour over the veal. Serve with lemon wedges to squeeze over the veal.
Serves 4

Variations
Veal with Lemon, Capers and Parsley – coat 2 veal escalopes in seasoned flour, then fry briskly in 2 tablespoons olive oil for about 1 minute each side. Transfer to warmed plates, cover and keep warm. Add 2 tablespoons each lemon juice and chopped parsley and 1 tablespoon capers, then whisk in 40 g (1½ oz) diced unsalted butter until the butter melts. Season and pour over the veal. **Serves 2**
Saltimbocca – lay a slice of prosciutto on each of 4 veal escalopes, scatter 2 shredded small sage leaves over each slice then roll up and secure with wooden cocktail sticks. Fry in a little olive oil and unsalted butter, until browned, then pour over about 125 ml (4 fl oz) medium-bodied dry white wine, allow to bubble for about 1 minute. Season with pepper and serve with lemon wedges. **Serves 4**

CHICKEN WITH GARLIC AND OREGANO

Oregano is a wild form of marjoram and the flavour can vary with the soil and climate; Greek oregano usually has a more robust flavour and so will withstand long, slow cooking. (Incidentally, rigani is the collective Greek name for a number of wild varieties of oregano and is not available fresh commercially.) Don't be put off by the amount of garlic used in this recipe or reduce it. During the long slow cooking, it mellows as it softens.

I CHICKEN WEIGHING ABOUT 1.75 KG (3½LB)

I LEMON

2-3 BULBS OF GARLIC, DIVIDED INTO CLOVES WITHOUT PEELING

I BUNCH OF OREGANO, DRIED, PREFERABLY IN A SUNNY WINDOW, FOR A FEW HOURS

250 ML (8 FL OZ) MEDIUM-BODIED DRY WHITE WINE

SALT AND PEPPER

Season the chicken inside and out. Thoroughly prick the lemon all over with a needle and put it inside the chicken. Put some of the garlic cloves and some of the oregano on the base of a heavy, deep, flameproof casserole in which the chicken will fit with just a little room to spare. Put the chicken into the casserole and tuck the remaining oregano and garlic around it. Pour over the wine and cover the casserole with greaseproof paper followed by a lid. Cook in a preheated oven, 200°C (400°F), Gas Mark 6, for 30 minutes, then lower the oven temperature to 180°C (350°F), Gas Mark 4, and cook for a further 1¼-1½ hours until the chicken is very tender.

Lift the chicken from the casserole and tip the juices from the cavity into the casserole. Place the chicken on a warmed serving dish and keep warm.

Discard the oregano from the casserole and remove and reserve the garlic. Tilt the casserole and spoon off the fat from the surface of the juices, then boil them to reduce to taste. Return the garlic to the sauce, then pour it into a warm sauceboat to serve with the chicken.

Serves 4

Variations

Quick Chicken with Garlic – boil garlic cloves in 3 separate changes of water. Purée the cloves and insert between the skin and flesh of chicken before grilling.

Chicken with Aïoli – either spread Aïoli (see page 24) between the flesh and skin of chicken portions before grilling, or serve Aïoli with the chicken.

VIBRANT DUCK WITH ORANGES AND OLIVES

This dish is a combination of Catalan and Valencian influences – Barbary-type duck from Catalonia and fruit from the lush groves of Valencia. Traditionally, a whole duck would be used, but I prefer to use duck breasts or portions, as they are more economical, produce less fat and are easier to serve. The fat removed from the duck before cooking is very good for frying, particularly potatoes and mushrooms; it just needs to be rendered down first.

4 DUCK BREASTS, EACH WEIGHING 175 G (6 OZ)

3 ORANGES

I LEMON

2 TABLESPOONS OLIVE OIL

I ONION, CHOPPED

3 CLOVES OF GARLIC, CRUSHED

50 G (2 OZ) RAW COUNTRY HAM, CHOPPED

2 TABLESPOONS BRANDY

175 ML (6 FL OZ) MEDIUM-BODIED DRY WHITE WINE

250 ML (8 FL OZ) CHICKEN STOCK

12 WHOLE BLACK OLIVES

SALT AND PEPPER

SPRIGS OF TARRAGON TO GARNISH

Remove the duck skin and excess fat. Cut the skin and pith from the oranges and lemon and slice the fruit thinly.

Heat the oil in a heavy flameproof casserole, add the duck breasts, two at a time, and fry until browned. Transfer to kitchen paper to drain. Stir the onion and garlic into the casserole and cook over a medium heat, stirring occasionally, until softened and lightly browned. Stir in the ham, brandy, white wine and stock to dislodge the sediment then add all the lemon slices, three quarters of the orange slices and the seasoning. Bring to the boil, bubble for a couple of minutes, then add the duck, turning the pieces over in the sauce. Cover and cook in a preheated oven, 180°C (350°F), Gas Mark 4, for about 50-60 minutes until the duck is quite tender.

Transfer the duck to a warmed serving plate, cover and keep warm in the oven with the heat turned off. Pass the cooking juices through a sieve into a saucepan, pressing down well on the fruit. Skim the fat from the surface of the liquid, then simmer until lightly thickened. Add the olives, adjust the seasoning and pour over the duck. Garnish with the remaining orange slices and tarragon.

Serves 4

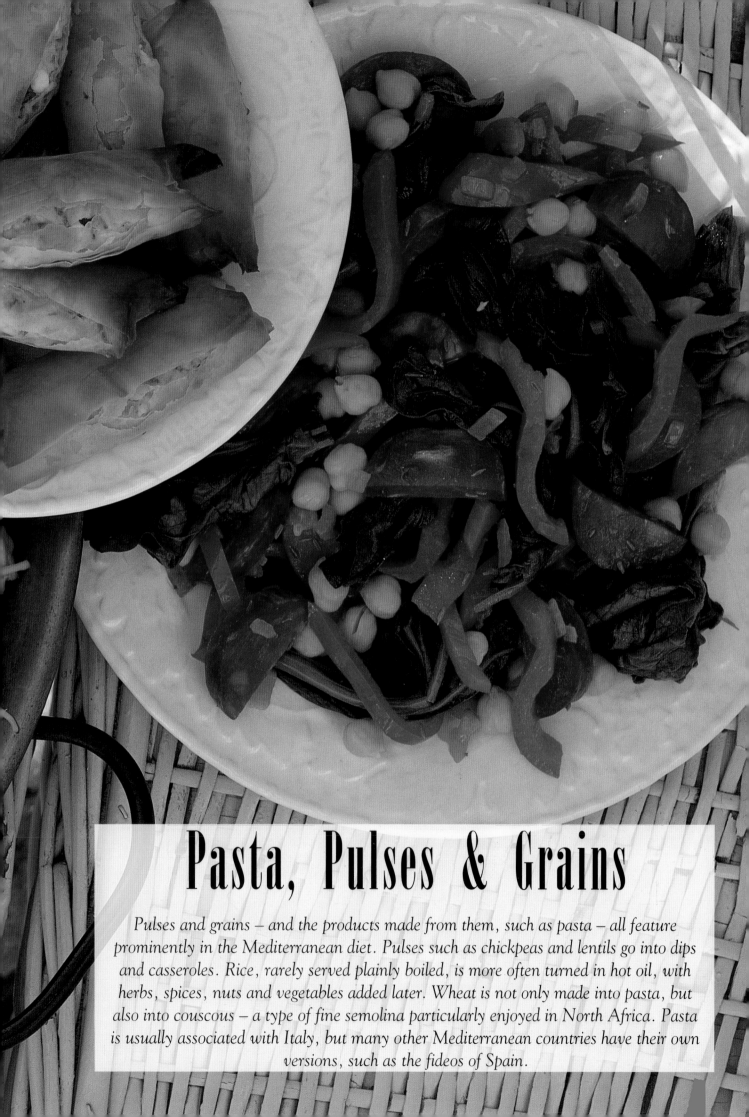

Pasta, Pulses & Grains

Pulses and grains – and the products made from them, such as pasta – all feature prominently in the Mediterranean diet. Pulses such as chickpeas and lentils go into dips and casseroles. Rice, rarely served plainly boiled, is more often turned in hot oil, with herbs, spices, nuts and vegetables added later. Wheat is not only made into pasta, but also into couscous – a type of fine semolina particularly enjoyed in North Africa. Pasta is usually associated with Italy, but many other Mediterranean countries have their own versions, such as the fideos of Spain.

CHICKPEAS WITH SPINACH

This sustaining, simple, inexpensive and well-flavoured recipe for a meal in a pot, exemplifies the type of dish that hungry, country-living Spanish families will tuck into during the winter. The original Spanish recipe included the traditional thickening of fried bread crushed with the garlic, but for the sake of lightness I leave it out.

250 G (8 OZ) CHICKPEAS, SOAKED OVERNIGHT, DRAINED AND RINSED

2½ TABLESPOONS OLIVE OIL

1 SPANISH ONION, FINELY CHOPPED

250 G (8 OZ) RAW CHORIZO, THICKLY SLICED (OPTIONAL)

2 LARGE RED PEPPERS, CORED, DESEEDED AND SLICED

1 TABLESPOON PAPRIKA

¼-½ TEASPOON CUMIN SEEDS, FINELY CRUSHED

500 G (1 LB) SPINACH, CHOPPED

3 CLOVES OF GARLIC

SALT AND PEPPER

Cook the chickpeas in 1½ times their volume of boiling water until tender, 1½-2 hours.

Meanwhile, heat 1½ tablespoons of the oil in a frying pan, add the onion and cook slowly, stirring occasionally, for 5 minutes. Add the chorizo, if used, and cook for a further 5-10 minutes until the onion is very soft. Stir in the red peppers and continue to cook, stirring occasionally, for about 10 minutes.

Heat the remaining oil in a saucepan, stir in the paprika and cumin seeds, add the spinach and cook until the spinach has wilted.

Using a pestle and mortar or the end of a rolling pin in a small bowl, pound the garlic with a pinch of salt.

Drain the chickpeas, reserving the liquid. Stir the chickpeas into the spinach with the onion mixture, the garlic mixture and 125 ml (4 fl oz) of chickpea liquid. Cover the pan and simmer for about 30 minutes, adding more liquid if necessary – the chickpeas should be quite moist.

Serves 4

Overleaf:
From left to right: Catalan Noodles with Seafood, Small Filo Pastries and Chickpeas with Spinach

CATALAN NOODLES WITH SEAFOOD

Pasta is an important feature of the Catalan diet: the local type, fideos, is 2.5-5 cm (1-2 inches) long and between vermicelli and spaghettini in thickness. It is typically cooked in a paella pan mixed with the other ingredients past the al dente stage, the cooking sometimes being completed in the oven– all of which is contrary to Italian practice.

4 CLOVES OF GARLIC, CHOPPED

1½ TABLESPOONS CHOPPED PARSLEY

4 TABLESPOONS OLIVE OIL

2 ONIONS, CHOPPED

3 TOMATOES, SKINNED, DESEEDED AND CHOPPED

1½ TEASPOONS PAPRIKA

375 G (12 OZ) SCORPION FISH, MONKFISH OR HALIBUT, CUT INTO PIECES

250 G (8 OZ) RAW KING PRAWNS IN THEIR SHELLS

250 G (8 OZ) RAW PRAWNS IN THEIR SHELLS

1.35 LITRES (2¼ PINTS) RICH FISH STOCK

275 G (9 OZ) DRIED FIDEOS, VERMICELLI OR SPAGHETTINI BROKEN INTO SHORT LENGTHS

LARGE PINCH OF SAFFRON THREADS, CRUSHED

CHOPPED PARSLEY TO GARNISH (OPTIONAL)

TO SERVE

AIOLI (SEE PAGE 24)

LEMON WEDGES

Pound garlic and parsley together. Heat 2 tablespoons of the oil in a cazuela or heavy flameproof earthenware casserole, add the onions and tomatoes, cook gently, until softened. Add the garlic and parsley mixture and paprika, continue to cook 2-3 minutes. Stir in all the seafood and coat. Add the stock, bring just to the boil, simmer gently for 5 minutes.

Meanwhile, heat the remaining oil in a large paella pan, add the fideos and stir over a moderate heat until light golden brown, but do not allow to scorch.

Remove the seafood from the cazuela and keep warm. Pour the contents of the cazuela on to the fideos, add the saffron and bring to the boil. Boil for 5 minutes, or until most of the liquid has been absorbed and the fideos are tender. Place the seafood on top, remove from the heat and leave covered by a thick cloth for a couple of minutes before sprinkling with a little parsley, if liked, and serving from the paella pan with Aïoli and lemon wedges.

Serves 4

SMALL FILO PASTRIES

Every Mediterranean country has its own version of and name for small savoury pastries – 'briks', 'boureks/boreks', 'brioutes', 'sambusak' – with various different shapes and fillings. The most common are cylindrical feta cheese ones and triangular spinach and feta.

APPROXIMATELY 500 G (1 LB) FILO PASTRY

OLIVE OIL FOR BRUSHING

CHEESE FILLING

375 G (12 OZ) FETA CHEESE

4 TABLESPOONS CHOPPED PARSLEY AND DILL

2 EGGS, BEATEN

PEPPER

SPINACH FILLING

1 KG (2 LB) FRESH SPINACH, STALKS REMOVED

125 G (4 OZ) EWES' MILK FETA CHEESE, CRUMBLED

FRESHLY GRATED NUTMEG

2 EGGS, BEATEN

SALT AND PEPPER

Cut each sheet of pastry into strips about 7 cm (3 inches) wide, stack on top of each other, cover with a damp cloth.

To make the cheese cylinders, mash the cheese with the herbs and pepper, then bind with the eggs. Brush a strip of pastry with oil, place a heaped teaspoon of filling at one end, then roll up for a few turns. Fold in the ends to seal in the filling, then continue to roll, without turning in the sides. Repeat with more strips until all the filling has been used. Place close together on a baking sheet.

To make spinach triangles, wash the spinach but do not dry, then cook in the water clinging to the leaves until wilted and surplus visible moisture has evaporated. Drain, squeeze to remove as much liquid as possible, then chop and mash with the remaining ingredients. Leave until cold.

Brush 1 of the remaining pastry strips with oil and place a heaped teaspoon of spinach filling at one end, about 2.5 cm (1 inch) from the side. Fold over one corner to make a triangle, then continue folding along the length of the pastry strip from side to side, keeping the shape of the triangle. Place side by side on a baking sheet.

Brush all the pastries with oil then bake in a preheated oven, 190°C (375°F), Gas Mark 5, for 10-15 minutes, rotating the shelves as necessary, until the pastries are golden and crisp. Serve warm.

Makes about 60

MUSSEL AND TOMATO PASTRIES

The markets in the Galatasaray district of Istanbul's old commercial and diplomatic area have some of the city's best street food. The mussel stalls are always popular: they offer shelled mussels threaded on small wooden skewers, dipped in a beer batter, deep-fried and served with garlicky tarator sauce or in a split chunk of fresh white bread, with a squeeze of lemon juice or crisp, plump yufka (filo pastry) cushions filled with the succulent Turkish mussels.

24 MUSSELS, SCRUBBED AND DEBEARDED

2 TABLESPOONS OLIVE OIL, PLUS EXTRA FOR BRUSHING

3 TOMATOES, SKINNED, DESEEDED AND CUT INTO 8 PIECES EACH

1 SMALL CLOVE OF GARLIC, CRUSHED

1½ TABLESPOONS LEMON JUICE

1½ TABLESPOONS FINELY CHOPPED PARSLEY

APPROXIMATELY 2 SHEETS OF FILO PASTRY

MELTED BUTTER OR BEATEN EGG FOR GLAZING

SALT AND PEPPER

Bring about 2.5 cm (1 inch) salted water to the boil in a large saucepan. Add the mussels, cover the pan and allow the mussels to steam for 2-3 minutes, tossing the pan frequently, until the shells open. Tip the mussels into a colander and discard any that remain closed. Remove the mussels from the shells.

Heat the oil in a saucepan over a low heat, add the tomatoes and simmer until soft. Drain through a sieve, retaining the juices and reserving the tomatoes. Pour the juices back into the saucepan, add the garlic and lemon juice and boil until syrupy. Cool, then add the tomatoes, mussels and seasoning.

Stack the sheets of pastry on top of each other, brushing each with oil. Cut into twelve 10 x 10 cm (4 x 4 inch) squares. Wet the edges. Spoon 2 mussels with some of the sauce on to each square, then fold the pastry over and press the edges together to seal. Oil a baking sheet and place the pastries on it. Glaze the tops with melted butter or beaten egg and bake in a preheated oven, 200°C (400°F), Gas Mark 6, for 10-12 minutes until golden. Carefully transfer to a wire rack. Eat warm or at room temperature.

Makes 12

PASTA WITH OLIVES, CAPERS AND ANCHOVIES

This is one of the charmingly robust, sun-packed local dishes that is served in the delightful restaurants near the port in the enchanting old town of Siracusa, the first settlement on Sicily. Sicilian cooking is based on the island's riches – fish, wheat made into memorable breads and pastas, a colourful profusion of vegetables, olives, capers, and special local cheeses, such as Pecorino Siciliano. This cheese can be eaten the day after it is made, so it is delicate, soft and creamy. Meat is not part of the Sicilian diet, but its absence passes unnoticed. The one-time Arab domination of the island is still very evident in the cooking; it is even said that 'itriiya', fusilli-like corkscrew tubes of pasta, were introduced by the Muslims. Traditionally, spaghetti is used, but I prefer to use bow ties, fusilli or another shape that will catch the particles in the sauce.

125 G (4 OZ) OIL-PACKED BLACK OLIVES, PITTED AND FINELY CHOPPED

8 ANCHOVY FILLETS, RINSED, DRIED AND CHOPPED

2 TABLESPOONS CAPERS PACKED IN SALT, RINSED

4 SUN-DRIED TOMATOES, SOAKED IF NECESSARY, CHOPPED QUITE FINELY

400 G (13 OZ) PASTA (SEE ABOVE)

5 TABLESPOONS VIRGIN OLIVE OIL

2 CLOVES OF GARLIC, FINELY CHOPPED

2 DRIED RED CHILLIES, CRUSHED

4 TABLESPOONS CHOPPED PARSLEY

SALT AND PEPPER

FRESHLY GRATED MATURE PECORINO SICILIANO OR

PECORINO SARDO CHEESE, TO SERVE

Mix together the olives, anchovies, capers, sun-dried tomatoes and black pepper.

Cook the pasta in a large saucepan in plenty of boiling salted water until just tender.

Meanwhile, heat the oil in a saucepan, add the garlic and chillies and cook until fragrant. Stir in the olive mixture and warm through.

Drain the pasta and tip into a warm serving bowl. Toss quickly with the olive mixture and the parsley and serve immediately with freshly grated Pecorino cheese.

Serves 4

ORECCHIETTE WITH PANCETTA AND BROCCOLI

Limpet shell-like orecchiette is the traditional pasta of Apulia. It is not easy to make domestically, as it is based on the local durum wheat and water, which produces a dough that is hard to work, and each piece has to be formed by hand. The shape makes it ideal for vegetable sauces.

375 G (12 OZ) FRESH BROCCOLI FLORETS

375 G (12 OZ) FRESH OR DRIED ORECCHIETTE

3 TABLESPOONS OLIVE OIL

50 G (2 OZ) PIECE OF PANCETTA, DICED

2 CLOVES OF GARLIC, CRUSHED

40 G (1½ OZ) PINE NUTS

SALT AND PEPPER

FRESHLY GRATED PECORINO CHEESE TO SERVE

Cook the broccoli in boiling water for 7-8 minutes, until just tender. Drain, refresh under cold water, then drain well.

Cook the pasta in plenty of boiling salted water until just tender, 6-7 minutes for fresh, or according to packet instructions for dried.

Meanwhile, heat the oil in a frying pan, add the pancetta and cook, stirring occasionally, until the pancetta is lightly browned, and adding the garlic towards the end. Add the nuts and heat until lightly toasted. Stir in the broccoli.

Drain the pasta, tip into a warm serving bowl and pour over the broccoli mixture. Season with salt and pepper. Toss quickly and serve with grated Pecorino cheese.

Serves 4

Top: Pasta with Olives, Capers and Anchovies
Bottom: Orecchiette with Pancetta and Broccoli

PAPPARDELLE WITH SCALLOPS AND PESTO

200 G (7 OZ) *DOPPIO ZERO* FLOUR, OR UNBLEACHED STRONG OR PLAIN FLOUR

2 EGGS, SIZE 2, BEATEN

I CLOVE OF GARLIC, CRUSHED

2 TABLESPOONS OLIVE OIL

16 SMALL SCALLOPS, OR 8 LARGE ONES, CORALS DETACHED AND WHITE BODIES CUT IN HALF HORIZONTALLY

I QUANTITY PESTO (SEE PAGE 23)

SALT AND PEPPER

I SUN-RIPENED TOMATO, DICED, SKINNED AND DESEEDED TO GARNISH

Sift the flour into a mound on a work surface and make a well in the centre. Pour in the eggs, add a generous pinch of salt, then draw the flour into the eggs to form a crumbly dough, using a fork at first, then your hand, and supporting the sides of the flour to prevent the egg running out.

Lightly flour the work surface and your hands and knead the dough by pushing it away from you with the heel of one hand, folding the dough back towards you, then turning the dough through 45 degrees. Repeat for about 10 minutes until the dough is smooth and elastic, changing hands and flouring them and the surface, as necessary. Alternatively, mix the dough in a food processor. Cover the dough with an upturned bowl and leave to rest for 30 minutes.

Roll the dough away from you, on a lightly floured surface using a floured rolling pin, rotating the dough through 45 degrees in between each stroke. Continue until the dough is 3 mm (⅛ inch) thick. Alternatively, use a pasta machine.

Leave the rolled out dough on a clean cloth to dry for a total of 30 minutes, allowing about one third of the sheet of dough to hang over the edge of the work surface for 10 minutes before turning it so another third is hanging over for 10 minutes; repeat with remaining third. The dough is ready to cut when the surface looks leathery. Fold the pasta sheet into a loose roll, cut across into 3 mm (⅛ inch) strips. Alternatively, use a pasta machine. Gently open out the rolls of pappardelle and leave to dry for about 5 minutes.

Add the pappardelle to a large saucepan of boiling water, stir, cover the saucepan and bring quickly to the boil. Uncover the pan and leave to boil for 4-6 minutes until just tender but firm to the bite. Meanwhile, heat the garlic in the oil in a frying pan until it is golden, then discard. Add the scallops to the remaining oil and fry for about 1 minute.

Drain the pasta and tip into a bowl, quickly add the Pesto and scallops and toss together. Serve garnished with tomato.

Serves 4

SPAGHETTI ALLA PUTTANESCA

Vibrant, racy, quick and obvious, this is a delicious pasta dish that exemplifies the character of its creators, the happy Neapolitans. 'Alla puttanesca' is not the most flattering of names though – it means 'in the manner of a prostitute', which is why you never see the dish given its English translation in recipes or on menus.

3 TABLESPOONS OLIVE OIL

2 CLOVES OF GARLIC, CRUSHED

I SMALL DRIED RED CHILLI, DESEEDED AND CHOPPED

6 ANCHOVY FILLETS, CHOPPED

500 G (I LB) WELL-FLAVOURED, RIPE TOMATOES, SKINNED, DESEEDED AND CHOPPED

125 G (4 OZ) PITTED BLACK OLIVES, HALVED

2 TABLESPOONS CAPERS

375 G (12 OZ) DRIED SPAGHETTI

SALT

In a saucepan, heat the oil, add the garlic, chilli and anchovies and cook for 1 minute. Stir in the tomatoes, olives, and capers, bring to the boil and simmer for about 20 minutes until thickened.

Cook the spaghetti in a large saucepan of boiling salted water until just tender. Drain, toss with the sauce and serve immediately.

Serves 4

FETTUCINE VERDE WITH GORGONZOLA SAUCE

In its original form, this recipe makes a rich and luxurious dish, but a lighter version can be made by beating 4 tablespoons ricotta cheese and substituting it for the cream.

400 G (13 OZ) FRESH OR DRIED FETTUCINE VERDE

1 TABLESPOON OLIVE OIL

1 ONION, FINELY CHOPPED

75 ML (3 FL OZ) MEDIUM-BODIED DRY WHITE WINE

175 G (6 OZ) GORGONZOLA CHEESE, CHOPPED

2-3 FRESH SAGE LEAVES

100 ML (3½ FL OZ) SINGLE CREAM

25 G (1 OZ) PARMESAN CHEESE, FRESHLY GRATED

SALT AND PEPPER

Bring a large saucepan of salted water to the boil, add the fettucine, stir, cover and return to the boil. Uncover and cook until the pasta is just tender, 5-7 minutes for fresh, or according to packet instructions for dried.

Meanwhile, heat the oil, add the onion and fry until soft. Add the wine and boil until reduced by half. Over a low heat, add the Gorgonzola and sage and stir frequently until smooth; do not allow to boil. Discard the sage and add the cream and pepper.

Drain the pasta thoroughly and return to the saucepan, pour over the sauce, toss well with the Parmesan cheese and serve immediately.

Serves 4

Variation

Fettucine with Gorgonzola and Walnuts – omit the sage leaves and toss the cooked pasta with 50-75 g (2-3 oz) chopped lightly toasted walnuts. Serve sprinkled with chopped parsley.

SPAGHETTI ALLA CARBONARA

Some people say that the name 'alla carbonara' is derived from the revolutionaries, called 'Carbonari', who worked for the unification of Italy. Others put forward the notion that it was invented by charcoal-makers, also called 'carbonari', since the ingredients were easily transportable and required very little cooking, so that the dish could be made on an open fire. The dish became internationally popular after homesick allies had 'adopted' it during World War II because it contained familiar bacon and eggs rather than an Italian-style tomato sauce.

3 TABLESPOONS OLIVE OIL

200 G (7 OZ) PIECE OF PANCETTA, SMOKED OR GREEN,

CUT INTO 2.5 CM (1 INCH) STRIPS

400 G (13 OZ) SPAGHETTI

3 EGG YOLKS

2 WHOLE EGGS, OR 4 WHOLE EGGS AND NO SEPARATE YOLKS (SEE ABOVE)

4 TABLESPOONS DOUBLE CREAM OR MASCARPONE (OPTIONAL)

50 G (2 OZ) PARMESAN CHEESE, FRESHLY GRATED

3 TABLESPOONS CHOPPED PARSLEY (OPTIONAL)

SALT AND PEPPER

Heat the oil in a frying pan, add the pancetta and cook, stirring occasionally, until brown and crisp.

Cook the spaghetti in plenty of boiling salted water until just tender.

Mix together the egg yolks, if used, eggs, cream or mascarpone, if used, cheese, parsley, if using, and pepper.

Drain the spaghetti, tip into a warm serving dish and immediately pour in the egg mixture and the contents of the frying pan. Toss together and serve.

Serves 4

FRAGRANT PILAF

Traditional recipes for pilafs usually specify soaking the rice, but while this may have been necessary at one time, with the rice now available I have found it makes no difference to the finished dish. Washing, however, is essential, as it removes surplus surface starch. Saffron will bring joy and happiness – or so folklore decrees – but even if it falls short on this count, it will definitely add a sunny colour and its own inimitable flavour and aroma.

250 G (8 OZ) BASMATI RICE

SEEDS FROM 4 CARDAMOM PODS, CRUSHED

LARGE PINCH OF SAFFRON THREADS, CRUSHED (OPTIONAL)

I CINNAMON STICK

1½ TEASPOONS CUMIN SEEDS

2 BAY LEAVES

I TABLESPOON OLIVE OIL

I ONION, CHOPPED

600 ML (I PINT) WATER

2 TABLESPOONS LEMON JUICE

75 G (3 OZ) RAISINS (OPTIONAL)

50 G (2 OZ) PINE NUTS, BROWNED IN OIL

SALT AND PEPPER

Wash the rice until the water runs clear. Put the cardamom seeds, saffron, cinnamon, cumin seeds and bay leaves in a large, heavy flameproof casserole and dry-fry over a moderate heat for 2-3 minutes until fragrant. Add the oil and when it is hot, stir in the onion and cook gently for about 10 minutes, stirring frequently, until it has softened and lightly browned. Add the rice, turning to coat the grains in the oil. Stir in the water, lemon juice, raisins, if used, and salt and pepper. Bring to the boil, cover and simmer for 15 minutes without lifting the lid, until the rice is just tender, all the water has been absorbed and small holes puncture the surface. Remove from the heat and leave, covered, for a few minutes. Fork through the pine nuts.

Serves 4

PAELLA WITH CHICKEN

The name of the dish paella comes directly from the name of the cooking utensil in which it is cooked. The original paella (the meal) came from Valencia and was made with rabbit, chicken, snails, various beans – and no fish. In Spain, paella is a festive dish and at the slightest excuse, families and groups of friends will hightail to the country or beach for an al fresco paella party – the ideal way to cook and enjoy a paella. An even heat under the whole surface of the base of the pan, preferably with some flames lapping slightly up the sides as they actually do affect the cooking (though perhaps this is making too fine a point), produces the best results. It is difficult to cook a paella for a number of people indoors – for 4-5 people you will need a 40 cm (16 inch) paella pan, for 6-8 a 50 cm (20 inch) one. It is very difficult to achieve the correct heat, as it is impossible to get the right even distribution of heat beneath the pan.

4 TABLESPOONS OLIVE OIL

I KG (2 LB) CHICKEN, CUT INTO SMALL PIECES

4 SMALL RABBIT PORTIONS

2 SPANISH ONIONS, CHOPPED

4 CLOVES OF GARLIC, CHOPPED

I TABLESPOON PAPRIKA

375 G (12 OZ) VALENCIAN OR RISOTTO RICE

3 EXTRA LARGE SUN-RIPENED TOMATOES, SKINNED, DESEEDED AND CHOPPED

1.8 LITRES (3 PINTS) BOILING CHICKEN STOCK

I SPRIG OF ROSEMARY

LARGE PINCH OF SAFFRON THREADS, FINELY CRUSHED

150 G (5 OZ) GREEN BEANS, CUT INTO SHORT LENGTHS

125 G (4 OZ) BROAD BEANS

SALT AND PEPPER

Heat the oil in a 40 cm (16 inch) paella pan or 4.2 litre (7 pint) wide shallow casserole. Add the chicken and rabbit, cook until lightly browned. Stir in the onion and garlic. Fry for 5 minutes, stir in the paprika followed by the rice. Stir 2-3 minutes, then stir in the tomatoes with all but 2 tablespoons of the stock, rosemary and salt and pepper. Dissolve the saffron in the reserved 2 tablespoons of stock, add to the paella and let boil 8-10 minutes without stirring.

Scatter the green beans and broad beans over the paella – do not stir. Gradually turn down the heat and simmer until the rice is tender and the liquid absorbed, 8-10 minutes. Cover the paella with a thick cloth, remove from the heat and leave for 5-10 minutes.

Serves 4

Clockwise from bottom:
Fragrant Pilaf, Paella with Chicken
and Cannellini Bean Salad

CANNELLINI BEAN SALAD

White, kidney-shaped cannellini beans feature in central Italian cooking, whereas rosy borlotti beans appear in recipes from northern and southern Italy. Of the many recipes using the beans, I particularly like this warm salad. As the flavour is at its height if the beans are tossed while hot and eaten while still warm, I time the cooking of the beans so that they can stand for 1 hour between dressing and serving. For the best flavour and texture, try to buy Italian beans from a good Italian food shop.

200 G (7 OZ) CANNELLINI BEANS, SOAKED OVERNIGHT

3 TABLESPOONS VIRGIN OLIVE OIL

2-3 ANCHOVY FILLETS, RINSED IF NECESSARY

YOLKS OF 2 HARD-BOILED EGGS

2 TABLESPOONS COARSELY CHOPPED ONION

1 TABLESPOON WHITE WINE VINEGAR OR LEMON JUICE

3 FRESH SAGE LEAVES

2 TABLESPOONS COARSELY CHOPPED PARSLEY

SALT AND PEPPER

Drain and rinse the beans. Place them in a heavy flameproof casserole with enough water just to cover. Bring to the boil over a medium heat for 10 minutes, cover and cook in a preheated oven, 160°C (325°F), Gas Mark 3, for 30 minutes, until tender. Keep an eye on the level of the water and pour in a little more if the beans become too dry, but there should be hardly any left at the end of the cooking.

In a food processor, purée the olive oil, anchovies, egg yolks, onion, vinegar or lemon juice, herbs, salt and pepper.

Drain the cannellini beans and tip them into a large bowl. Pour over the sauce and toss gently until the beans are well coated. Leave at room temperature for 1 hour, then toss again just before serving.

Serves 4

Variation

Tuscan Fagioli all'Uccelletto – Cook 325 g (11 oz) soaked and drained cannellini beans as above. Fry 5 sage leaves and 2 crushed cloves of garlic in 3 tablespoons virgin olive oil in a shallow earthenware dish until the garlic begins to colour. Stir in the beans and cook for about 5 minutes before adding 500 g (1 lb) skinned, deseeded and chopped well-flavoured tomatoes, salt and pepper. Cover and cook over a moderate heat for about 20 minutes.

FUSILLI WITH FRESH MIXED HERBS

This is one of my favourite pasta dishes – it is simple and light, yet wonderfully sustaining because there is so much fresh, satisfying flavour trapped within the spirals of pasta.

400 G (13 OZ) FUSILLI

2 TABLESPOONS OLIVE OIL

250 G (8 OZ) RICOTTA CHEESE

2 TABLESPOONS CHOPPED THYME

2 TABLESPOONS CHOPPED PARSLEY

1 TABLESPOON CHOPPED OREGANO

1 TABLESPOON CHOPPED MINT

1 TABLESPOON SHREDDED BASIL

1 SMALL CLOVE OF GARLIC, FINELY CHOPPED

SALT AND PEPPER

FRESHLY GRATED PECORINO CHEESE TO SERVE

Cook the fusilli in a large saucepan of boiling salted water until just tender, about 9 minutes.

Meanwhile, beat the oil into the ricotta cheese, then add the herbs, garlic and seasoning.

Drain the pasta in a colander but leave a little of the cooking water clinging to thin down the sauce. Tip the pasta into a warm serving dish and toss with the herb mixture. Serve with grated Pecorino cheese.

Serves 4

BAKED LASAGNE WITH MEAT AND BECHAMEL SAUCES

Baking is the most usual way of cooking lasagne, and layered with minced meat and béchamel sauces the most widely known (and bastardized) way of baking it (indeed, the dish is frequently referred to simply as 'lasagne'). Nevertheless, there are many other ways: both traditional regional ones and modern. In the south, lasagne is layered with local sausage, small meatballs, mozzarella cheese, ricotta cheese and hard-boiled eggs, all generously sauced with a classic Neopolitan ragu, a meat sauce. Elsewhere, chicken livers, mushrooms, brains and sweetbreads may be included. Modern lasagne dishes contain fish and vegetables. The secrets of producing good 'lasagne' are cooking the ragu slowly and gently, and flavouring the béchamel sauce. Both sauces can be made in advance.

250 G (8 OZ) LASAGNE VERDE OR READY-TO-USE LASAGNE

65 G (2½ OZ) PARMESAN CHEESE, FRESHLY GRATED

SALT AND PEPPER

RAGU

1½ TABLESPOONS OLIVE OIL

40 G (1½ OZ) PANCETTA OR BACON, FINELY CHOPPED

I SMALL ONION, FINELY CHOPPED

I LARGE CLOVE OF GARLIC, FINELY CHOPPED

½ SMALL CARROT, FINELY CHOPPED

I SMALL STICK OF CELERY, FINELY CHOPPED

125 ML (4 FL OZ) MEDIUM-BODIED DRY WHITE WINE

275 G (9 OZ) LEAN BEEF, MINCED

4 TABLESPOONS MILK

300 G (10 OZ) EXTRA LARGE SUN-RIPENED TOMATOES, CHOPPED

I TABLESPOON TORN BASIL

BECHAMEL SAUCE

750 ML (1¼ PINTS) MILK

½ ONION

PIECE OF CARROT

6 BLACK PEPPERCORNS

I BAY LEAF

FRESHLY GRATED NUTMEG

75 G (3 OZ) UNSALTED BUTTER

50 G (2 OZ) PLAIN FLOUR

For the ragu, heat the oil in a small, heavy casserole, preferably earthenware, add the pancetta or bacon, onion, garlic, carrot and celery and cook, stirring occasionally, until the onion and garlic have softened but not coloured. Stir in the wine and allow to bubble gently until almost evaporated, then stir in the meat, breaking up the pieces with a fork. Cook gently until it turns a whitish grey colour, then stir in the milk and continue to cook gently, stirring frequently, until the milk has evaporated. Stir in the tomatoes and seasoning to taste, heat almost to simmering point, cover and cook very gently for about 1 hour, stirring frequently. Uncover and continue to cook until there is no free liquid and the sauce is concentrated. Stir in the basil.

To make the béchamel sauce, gently heat the milk with the vegetables, peppercorns, bay leaf and nutmeg, until it comes to the boil. Remove from the heat, cover, leave for 15 minutes, then strain. Melt the butter in a heavy-bottomed saucepan, stir in the flour and cook for about 30 seconds. Over a low heat, slowly pour in the milk, stirring constantly, then bring to the boil, stirring. Simmer for about 5 minutes, stirring occasionally. Remove from the heat and season to taste with salt and pepper.

If not using ready-to-use lasagne, bring a large saucepan of salted water to the boil, add the lasagne, stir, cover and return to the boil. If using fresh lasagne, boil for 3 minutes, if using dried, 7-8 minutes. Do not overcook or it will be soggy. Drain well and rinse under cold running water. If using pre-cooked ready-to-use lasagne, follow packet instructions for further information.

Spread about one quarter of the ragu evenly over the bottom of a large shallow baking dish, about 18 x 24 cm (7 x 9½ inches). Cover with approximately one quarter of the béchamel sauce, then arrange a single layer of lasagne on top. Repeat with the remaining ingredients finishing with a layer of béchamel sauce. Cover this with Parmesan cheese and bake in a preheated oven, 180°C (350°F), Gas Mark 4, for about 30-35 minutes.

Serves 4-6

RICE WITH BROAD BEANS

Cooking fresh broad beans and some of the coriander along with the rice gives this Egyptian dish its special flavour, but if this ideal is not possible, the recipe can be made using thawed frozen broad beans. If you are using these, quickly add them to the rice after it has been cooking for 10 minutes and immediately cover the saucepan again.

250 G (8 OZ) BASMATI RICE

6 SPRING ONIONS, CUT INTO 2.5 CM (1 INCH) LENGTHS

2 TABLESPOONS OLIVE OIL

375 G (12 OZ) SHELLED BROAD BEANS

600 ML (1 PINT) WATER

4 TABLESPOONS CHOPPED CORIANDER

SALT AND PEPPER

SPLIT ALMONDS, TOASTED, TO GARNISH

GREEK EWES' MILK YOGURT TO SERVE

Rinse the rice until the water runs clear.

Meanwhile, gently cook the spring onions in the oil in a heavy saucepan, stirring, for 2-3 minutes.

Add the rice and beans and cook, stirring, until the rice is transparent. Stir in the water, half the coriander and salt and pepper. Bring to the boil, then cover tightly and simmer for about 15 minutes, without lifting the lid, until the rice is tender and the liquid almost absorbed. Remove from the heat and leave, covered, for a few minutes. Fork through the remaining coriander and serve garnished with toasted almonds and accompanied by yogurt.

Serves 4

POLENTA

Golden yellow polenta, made from coarsely ground cornmeal, used to be a staple food of the poor in northern Italy. Traditionally, a large copper pot, a paiolo, was kept above the open fire, specifically for cooking polenta, and a spoon was kept for stirring the porridge-like mass during the long, slow cooking process. The authentic way of adding raw polenta to the liquid is in a thin stream, but as this runs the risk of becoming lumpy, I usually blend the meal with water first. To eliminate the very frequent stirring needed during cooking, the cooking can be done in a water bath. 'Instant' polenta that is ready in about 5 minutes is also available. Cheese such as Parmesan, mozzarella or fontina, and butter can be mixed in at end of cooking, if liked, and the polenta served as it is with meat, poultry or Italian sausages. It may be spread in a baking dish, cooled then baked with a topping of cheese, sliced and toasted or fried and spread with pesto or tapenade.

250 G (8 OZ) POLENTA

1.5 LITRES (2½ PINTS) WATER

UNSALTED BUTTER AND/OR PARMESAN CHEESE TO TASTE AND

ACCORDING TO HOW THE POLENTA IS TO BE SERVED

SALT AND PEPPER

Mix together the polenta and about 300 ml (½ pint) water. Bring the remaining water to a boil in a heavy saucepan. Stir in the polenta paste. Keep stirring until the mixture comes to the boil again, then cook, stirring very frequently, until the mixture comes away from the saucepan; this will take about 25 minutes. Place the saucepan in another saucepan filled with boiling water, cover and cook, stirring occasionally, for 30-45 minutes, or until the polenta thickens.

Add butter and/or Parmesan cheese, and season to taste.

To cut polenta into shapes for grilling or frying, spread it to a depth of about 1-2 cm (½-¾ inches) in a shallow dish that has been rinsed with cold water. Leave until cold and set, then cut into the required shapes and either brush with olive oil and grill until a crust forms, or fry in butter.

Serves 4

Variation
Gorgonzola Polenta Crostini – mash 125 g (4 oz) Gorgonzola cheese with 50 g (2 oz) mascarpone, spread over polenta slices, grill until just bubbling, about 2 minutes, sprinkle with chopped toasted walnuts and serve hot.

Polenta

RISOTTO IN BIANCO

This method has been devised perfectly to match the local rice, a medium grain one that absorbs liquid and so swells when cooked without becoming mushy. The prime rice to look for is carnaroli, but arborio is the one you are most likely to find. Risottos can be flavoured with many different ingredients, but all follow the procedure given below.

1 ONION, FINELY CHOPPED

65 G (2½ OZ) UNSALTED BUTTER

300 G (10 OZ) CARNAROLI OR ARBORIO RICE

1.2 LITRES (2 PINTS) GOOD QUALITY STOCK, BROUGHT TO THE BOIL

50 G (2 OZ) PARMESAN CHEESE, FRESHLY GRATED

SALT (OPTIONAL)

GRATED PARMESAN CHEESE TO SERVE (OPTIONAL)

In a heavy saucepan, cook the onion in half of the butter until translucent. Stir in the rice with a wooden spoon and cook, stirring, for 1-2 minutes until it is well coated and has absorbed the butter. Over a moderate heat, stir in about 150 ml (¼ pint) of the boiling stock and continue to cook at a steady, but not too violent bubble, stirring constantly, until there is no free liquid and the rice is creamy. Stir in a further 150 ml (¼ pint) or so of the boiling stock, but do not drown the rice. Continue to cook the risotto, adding gradually smaller quantities of the boiling stock until the rice is soft outside but firm within, creamy and bound together, neither moist nor dry; this should take about 15-20 minutes altogether.

Remove the pan from the heat, stir in the remaining butter, diced, and the cheese. Cover and leave 1 minute for the butter to be absorbed. Stir, taste and add salt, if necessary. Serve immediately with extra cheese, if liked.

Serves 4

Variations

Risotto with Courgettes and Thyme – use 1 small onion, 50 g (2 oz) unsalted butter, 200 g (7 oz) rice, 400 ml (14 fl oz) stock plus 250 g (9 oz) sliced small courgettes, 1 sprig of thyme and 50 ml (2 fl oz) dry white wine; add the wine just before the end of the cooking.

Asparagus Risotto – add 400 g (13 oz) cooked asparagus spears, cut into 1 cm (½ inch) lengths, and use the asparagus cooking liquid as part of the stock for cooking the rice. Incorporate the asparagus into the rice with the last addition of stock.

BURGHUL PILAF WITH AUBERGINE AND CHEESE

Burghul pilafs can be made more quickly and easily than their rice counterpart, and make an interesting change. This is one of my favourites.

1 AUBERGINE, CUT INTO 2.5 CM (1 INCH) CUBES

2 TABLESPOONS OLIVE OIL

250 G (8 OZ) BURGHUL

250 ML (8 FL OZ) WATER

75-125 G (3-4 OZ) HALUMI CHEESE, CUT INTO SMALL CUBES

SALT AND PEPPER

CORIANDER LEAVES OR SHREDDED BASIL TO GARNISH

Put the aubergine into a colander, sprinkle with salt and leave for 30-60 minutes. Rinse well and pat dry.

Heat the oil, add the aubergine and fry for several minutes until tender, stirring occasionally. Using a slotted spoon, transfer to kitchen paper to drain.

Pour the oil from the pan. Add the burghul and water to the pan, cover and simmer for 5 minutes.

Stir in the aubergines, and heat through, covered, for a few minutes. Scatter the cheese over the top, grind over black pepper, cover the pan and leave off the heat for a few minutes so the cheese begins to melt.

Serve immediately, garnished with coriander or, unconventionally, basil.

Serves 4

SPANOKOPITTA

A good version of this typical, popular Greek pie has crisp pastry, although not too much in relation to the filling.

2 TABLESPOONS OLIVE OIL, PLUS EXTRA FOR BRUSHING

I ONION, FINELY CHOPPED

I BUNCH SPRING ONIONS, FINELY CHOPPED

I KG (2 LB) FRESH SPINACH, STALKS REMOVED

2 LARGE EGGS, BEATEN

175 G (6 OZ) EWES' MILK FETA CHEESE, CRUMBLED

1½ TABLESPOONS FRESHLY GRATED KEFALOTIRI OR PARMESAN CHEESE

3 TABLESPOONS CHOPPED PARSLEY

1½ TABLESPOONS CHOPPED DILL

APPROXIMATELY 10 SHEETS FILO PASTRY

SALT AND PEPPER

Heat the oil, add the onion and spring onions and cook, stirring occasionally, until softened but not coloured. Wash but do not dry the spinach, then chop and stir into the onions, cook until wilted and all visible liquid has evaporated.

Remove from the heat, cool slightly and stir in the eggs, cheeses, parsley, dill, plenty of black pepper and a little salt, if necessary – the cheeses are salty anyway.

Brush a 28 x 18 cm (11 x 7 inch) baking dish with oil. Line with a sheet of filo, trimming it so it overhangs by 2.5-5 cm (1-2 inches). Brush with oil then cover with another sheet of filo. Repeat with 3 more sheets of filo. Cover the unused sheets of filo with a damp cloth. Add the spinach mixture to the dish and spread it evenly to the sides. Layer the remaining filo in the dish as before, trimming the pastry edges to fit the dish exactly. Fold the corners and edges of the bottom sheets over the top and brush well with oil or butter to seal. Brush the top generously with oil and score through the top 2 or 3 layers of pastry with the point of a sharp knife to make a diamond pattern.

Bake in a preheated oven, 180°C (350°F), Gas Mark 4, for about 40 minutes until crisp and golden. Serve warm or at room temperature – do not chill.

Serves 4

Variation

Turkish Leek Pie – for the filling, substitute 4 plump leeks for the spinach. Halve the leeks lengthways, sprinkle sparingly with a little salt and leave in a colander for about 20 minutes until the leeks are limp. Squeeze well to expel surplus moisture. Mix with the eggs, cheeses, 3 tablespoons chopped parsley and a pinch of hot paprika or cayenne; do not add salt because of the salt used for the leeks.

GREEK COURGETTE PICNIC PIE

On the Greek islands, large picnics and family gatherings are de rigeur after Mass on Easter Sunday and Monday. Portable pastries, such as this recipe, are an obvious choice for these occasions. The yogurt and light olive oil in this pastry make it crisp and light with a delicious flavour (and, incidentally, ideal for anyone worried about cholesterol). Add a well-matched filling of courgettes, cheese and herbs and you have a pie that any true Greek would be delighted to take to the picnic.

190 G (6½ OZ) SELF-RAISING FLOUR

6 TABLESPOONS GREEK STRAINED EWES' MILK YOGURT

4 TABLESPOONS OLIVE OIL PLUS EXTRA FOR BRUSHING

SALT AND PEPPER

FILLING

I KG (2 LB) SMALL COURGETTES, COARSELY GRATED

I ONION, COARSELY GRATED

2 CLOVES OF GARLIC, CHOPPED

2 TABLESPOONS OLIVE OIL

125 G (4 OZ) GREEK MIZITHRA CHEESE, OR EWES' MILK FETA CHEESE

4 EGGS, LIGHTLY BEATEN

50 G (2 OZ) KEFALOTIRI OR PARMESAN CHEESE, FRESHLY GRATED

4 TABLESPOONS MIXED CHOPPED PARSLEY, DILL AND MINT

Toss the courgettes with salt, put in a colander, cover with a weighted plate and leave for 1 hour to drain.

To make the pastry, sift the flour and a little salt and pepper into a bowl. Make a well in the centre, slowly add the yogurt and olive oil, stirring in the seasoned flour to make a smooth dough. Cover and leave in the refrigerator for 15 minutes.

Rinse the courgettes, dry well and sauté with the onion and garlic in the oil until just softened. Mix with the remaining filling ingredients.

Oil a 23 cm (9 inch) loose-bottomed, deep flan tin. On a lightly floured surface, roll out the dough and use to line the flan tin. Prick the base with a fork and line with greaseproof paper and baking beans. Bake in a preheated oven, 200°C (400°F), Gas Mark 6, for 10-15 minutes. Lower the oven temperature to 190°C (375°F), Gas Mark 5. Remove the beans and greaseproof paper from the pastry case.

Stir the filling, pour into the pastry and bake for about 25 minutes until the filling is just set and lightly browned. Serve warm or cold.

Serves 6

Bread

Each country has its own repertoire of bread recipes. When making any of the following recipes, except pitta bread, you can imitate the conditions of a traditional brick oven by baking the bread on either a baking stone or unglazed quarry tiles – inexpensive and easily available from a builder's merchant. The baking stones or quarry tiles must be preheated for at least 15 minutes before the dough is transferred to the stone or tiles, using a floured 'peel' or paddle or a sheet of thin, but firm cardboard.

OLIVE BREAD

Greek olive bread, 'elioti' or 'eliopitta', originated as a Lenten food for members of the Eastern Orthodox Church. Containing two staples of the Mediterranean diet – olives and bread – elioti provided a major source of nourishment. Do not use olives that have been steeped in vinegar.

10 G (⅓ OZ) FRESH YEAST OR 1¼ TEASPOONS EASY-BLEND YEAST

PINCH OF SUGAR

APPROXIMATELY 300 ML (½ PINT) WARM WATER

500 G (1 LB) UNBLEACHED STRONG WHITE FLOUR

2 TEASPOONS CHOPPED OREGANO

3 TABLESPOONS OLIVE OIL PLUS EXTRA FOR BRUSHING

150 G (5 OZ) OIL-STEEPED BLACK OLIVES, PITTED

SALT

Blend the fresh yeast, if used, with the sugar in a little of the water then leave until frothy.

Sieve the flour and a pinch of salt into a bowl. Stir in the easy-blend yeast, if used, and oregano. Form a well in the centre then slowly pour in the yeast liquid, if used, the remaining water and the oil, drawing in the dry ingredients to make a dough. Turn the dough on to a floured surface and knead for 5-7 minutes. Place the dough in a clean bowl, cover and leave at room temperature until doubled in bulk.

Tip the dough on to a floured surface and knead again for about 2 minutes, working in the olives. Divide the dough into 4, form into balls and place well apart on 2 oiled baking sheets, pressing them down gently. Cover with a damp cloth and leave to rise again for about 25 minutes.

Brush the loaves with water to soften the crusts and bake in a preheated oven, 230°C (450°F), Gas Mark 8, for 30 minutes until the top is golden and they sound hollow when tapped underneath.

Makes 4 small loaves

Overleaf:
From left to right: Round Flat Bread,
Olive Bread and Country Bread

ROUND FLAT BREAD

Pitta-style flat breads are eaten throughout the Middle East and eastern Mediterranean. They can be flavoured with ground cumin or herbs, or brushed after shaping with olive oil and sprinkled with sesame seeds or grated Parmesan. To obtain the characteristic hollow, puffed shape, a very hot oven is necessary. I also recommend preheating the baking trays for 2 minutes first. Alternatively, you can cook the breads under a very hot grill.

15 G (½ OZ) FRESH YEAST OR 1½ TEASPOONS EASY-BLEND YEAST

APPROXIMATELY 275 ML (9 FL OZ) WARM WATER

500 G (1 LB) UNBLEACHED STRONG WHITE FLOUR

SALT

1 TABLESPOON OLIVE OIL

Blend the fresh yeast, if using, with a little of the water and leave until frothy.

Sieve the flour and a pinch of salt into a bowl. Stir in the easy-blend yeast, if used. Form a well in the centre. Pour in the yeast liquid, if used, remaining water and the oil and gradually draw the dry ingredients into the liquids, first using a wooden spoon, then your hand. Mix to a firm, soft dough.

Turn the dough on to a lightly floured surface, knead for about 15 minutes until smooth and elastic. Place in a clean bowl, cover and leave at room temperature until doubled in bulk.

Turn the dough on to the work surface and knead briefly. Divide into 12 pieces. Flatten each piece to about 5 mm (¼ inch) thick and 10 cm (4 inches) in diameter. Brush with oil, place well apart on baking sheets. Cover with a lightly floured cloth, leave to rise for about 20 minutes.

Dampen the top of each dough piece with water to prevent browning. If cooking in the oven, transfer pieces to an oiled, preheated baking tray and bake in a preheated oven, 260°C (500°F), Gas Mark 10, or the highest possible temperature, for 3 minutes, then reduce temperature to 230°C (450°F), Gas Mark 8, and bake a further 2-3 minutes until puffed up and lightly speckled brown. If grilling, place the pieces under a preheated very hot grill, cook until puffed up and speckled brown. Turn over immediately and leave for another minute.

Seal bread that is not to be eaten straight away in a plastic bag while it is still warm. For longer storage, freeze it, then reheat from frozen under the grill or in the oven. Bread that becomes dry can be refreshed by sprinkling with water and warming under a preheated grill or in the oven. To keep several breads hot, wrap them in foil and put in the oven.

Makes about 12

COUNTRY BREAD

Long, slow rising produces a loaf with a better texture than a quicker risen one and allows less yeast to be used, which gives an improved flavour. After you have eaten bread made in this way for a while, the yeastiness of almost every other bread becomes very apparent and unpleasant. Putting a hot baking tin filled with boiling water into the oven at the same time as the unbaked loaf helps to give a good crust. The bread can be flavoured and enriched by adding about 3 tablespoons olive oil at the final kneading stage.

10 G (⅓ OZ) FRESH YEAST OR 2 TEASPOONS DRIED YEAST

APPROXIMATELY 300 ML (½ PINT) WARM WATER

PINCH OF SUGAR IF USING DRY YEAST

500 G (1 LB) STRONG FLOUR

PINCH OF SALT

3 TABLESPOONS OLIVE OIL (OPTIONAL)

To make the 'sponge', blend or dissolve the yeast in 5 tablespoons of the warm water, plus the sugar if using dried yeast. Put about 50 g (2 oz) of the flour into a bowl, pour over the yeast liquid and mix to a smooth ball of dough. Turn on to a floured work surface and knead together.

Put 250 g (8 oz) of the remaining flour into a bowl. Place the dough on top and cover with the remaining flour. Cover the bowl with a cloth, wrap in a towel and leave overnight.

With a wooden spoon, carefully draw together the ingredients in the bowl, slowly pouring in the remaining water and adding the salt and oil, if used. As more water is added, use your hand for mixing to make a light elastic dough.

Transfer the dough to a floured work surface and knead well for about 15 minutes. Return the dough to the bowl, cover and leave to rise slowly until doubled in bulk.

Turn the dough on to the work surface, knead lightly and briefly, then form into a round or long loaf. Flour a baking sheet and place the loaf on it. Spray with water and leave until doubled in bulk. Put the bakestone or quarry tiles, if used, and a baking tin in the oven to heat for 20 minutes.

Transfer the loaf to the bakestone or quarry tiles, if used. With the point of a sharp knife, cut 3 x 1 cm (½ inch) deep slashes in the loaf, then put it in a preheated oven, 230°C (450°F), Gas Mark 8, and fill the baking tin with boiling water. Immediately close the oven and bake the loaf for about 15 minutes. Reduce the oven temperature to 190°C (375°F), Gas Mark 5, and bake for a further 15-20 minutes until the loaf sounds hollow when tapped on the base. Transfer to a wire rack to cool.

Serves 4

PISSALADIERE

Pissaladière is popular all along the Provençal coast. The name comes from 'pissalat', the anchovy paste that used to be spread on the dough, but which has been superseded by strips of anchovy fillets.

DOUGH

250 G (8 OZ) UNBLEACHED STRONG WHITE FLOUR

1 TEASPOON EASY-BLEND YEAST

1 TEASPOON SALT

1 TABLESPOON MIXED PROVENCAL HERBS

175 ML (6 FL OZ) WARM WATER

OLIVE OIL, FOR BRUSHING

FILLING

4 TABLESPOONS OLIVE OIL

1 KG (2 LB) LARGE ONIONS, THINLY SLICED

2 CLOVES OF GARLIC, THINLY SLICED

SALT AND PEPPER

TOPPING

12 ANCHOVY FILLETS IN OIL

24 NICOISE OLIVES

1 TABLESPOON MIXED PROVENCAL HERBS

To make the dough, stir together the flour, yeast, salt, herbs and a little pepper. Form a well in the centre, then slowly pour in the water, stirring in the dry ingredients to form a smooth dough. Knead well. Place in a clean bowl, cover and leave at room temperature until doubled in bulk.

Make the filling. Heat the oil in a heavy-bottomed frying pan, add the onions and garlic and cook over a low heat, stirring occasionally, for about 30 minutes until the onions are very soft and beginning to show signs of sticking to the pan. Remove from the heat and add the seasonings. Tip into a sieve to drain.

Turn the dough on to a lightly floured surface and roll out to just over 33 x 23 cm (13 x 9 inches). Using the rolling pin, carefully transfer the dough to an oiled 33 x 23 cm (13 x 9 inch) Swiss roll tin, pushing it well into the corners and up the sides. Brush the surface with olive oil, cover and leave in a warm place for 20-30 minutes until slightly risen.

Spread the onion over the dough. Drain the anchovies, reserving the oil. Slice each fillet in half lengthways, arrange in a lattice pattern over the onion. Strew the olives on top, sprinkle with herbs, brush with the oil from the anchovies. Bake on the top shelf of a preheated oven, 220°C (425°F), Gas Mark 7, for 20-30 minutes. Serve hot, warm or cold.

Serves 2-4

FOCACCIA

Originally Focaccia was baked on a stone or terracotta slab under hot ashes in the hearth. Later the dough was baked in large copper tins in a brick oven with glowing twigs surrounding the tin. Focaccia may be flavoured in many different ways, whether crackling with crunchy coarse salt, studded with black olives, almost oozing with rich-flavoured olive oil, scented with herbs, topped with melting, savoury onions or combined with crisp diced bacon. In the fishing village of Recco, between Genoa and Santa Margherita, the local soft cows' cheese is sandwiched between two layers of dough, the top one being so thin it is almost transparent. There are also some sweet versions. Focaccia is eaten as a snack, served as antipasti with cheese or to accompany a meal, and is ideal for picnics. Because of the oil it contains, the dough is easy to work.

10 G (⅓ OZ) FRESH YEAST, OR 2 TEASPOONS DRIED YEAST

APPROXIMATELY 300 ML (½ PINT) WARM MILK

500 G (1 LB) UNBLEACHED STRONG WHITE FLOUR

3-5 TABLESPOONS VIRGIN OLIVE OIL, PLUS EXTRA FOR BRUSHING

COARSE SEA SALT

Blend or dissolve the yeast with the milk and leave until frothy. Sieve the flour into a large bowl, stir in a little salt and make a well in the centre. Slowly pour in the yeast liquid and oil, stirring the dry ingredients into the liquid to make a smooth, soft but not wet dough; add a little more milk if necessary. Turn on to a floured surface and knead until smooth and elastic. Place the dough in a clean bowl, cover and leave at room temperature until doubled in bulk.

Flour a baking sheet. Tip the dough on to a floured surface and knead for 2-3 minutes. Roll the dough into a large circle about 5-10 mm (¼-½ inch) thick – the thicker it is, the chewier the bread. Carefully transfer the dough to the baking sheet, keeping the circular shape. Brush with olive oil and sprinkle over coarse salt. With the end of a wooden spoon or a clean finger make deep indentations over the surface of the dough. Spray with water and leave until doubled in bulk. Put the bakestone or quarry tiles, if used, and a baking tin in the oven to heat for 20 minutes.

Transfer the loaf to the bakestone or quarry tiles, if used. Put loaf in a preheated oven, 200°C (400°F), Gas Mark 6, and fill the baking tin with hot water. Immediately close the oven door and bake loaf for 15-20 minutes if 5 mm (¼ inch) thick, 20-25 minutes if slightly thicker, until golden and the underneath sounds hollow when tapped. Serve warm.

Serves 4

Variations

Focaccia with Herbs – knead 10 or 12 torn fresh sage leaves or 2 teaspoons rosemary leaves into the dough at the second kneading. Shape and leave to rise as before, brush with an extra tablespoon of olive oil before baking.

Focaccia with Sun-dried Tomatoes – add about 30 g (1¼ oz) chopped sun-dried tomatoes kept in oil to the dough before the final shaping; use the oil from the tomatoes in the dough.

Gorgonzola Focaccia – add 175 g (6 oz) chopped Gorgonzola cheese to the dough before the final shaping.

Cheese-Filled Focaccia – after the second rising, halve the dough; use 1 piece to line a 37.5 x 25 cm (15 x 10 inch) oiled Swiss roll tin, leaving a slight overhang. Cover the surface with 500 g (1 lb) sliced stracchino or other soft melting cheese, leaving a 2.5 cm (1 inch) border. Cover with the remaining dough, folding the bottom overhang over to seal the edge. Sprinkle with coarse salt, then bake for 30 minutes at 200°C (400°F), Gas Mark 6. Cool for 5 minutes before cutting.

Tomato and Anchovy-Filled Focaccia – soften 2 chopped onions and 2 garlic cloves in olive oil, but do not allow to colour. Add 750 g (1½ lb) skinned, deseeded and chopped sun-ripened tomatoes, 4 sun-dried tomato halves, 2 tablespoons capers and 1 tablespoon oregano and simmer until thick. Leave to cool. Roll out half the dough to a 30 cm (12 inch) circle, place on an oiled baking sheet and spread with the tomato mixture, leaving a 2.5 cm (1 inch) border. Arrange 12 anchovy fillets on top, scatter over 75 g (3 oz) pitted oil-cured black olives, then 150-175 g (5-6 oz) coarsely grated mozzarella. Cover with the remaining dough and seal the edges. Bake at 220°C (425°F), Gas Mark 7, for 30 minutes until risen and golden. Serve warm.

*Clockwise from top right:
Goats' Cheese, Tomato and Pesto Pizza,
Focaccia and Pissaladière*

PIZZA

In colloquial Italian, a 'pizza' is almost any kind of pie, savoury or sweet, open or covered and made from any type of pastry or yeast dough. The concept of adding savoury ingredients to bread dough has been around since the earliest days of breadmaking, but the pizza as we know it today was the creation of the Neopolitans during the eighteenth century, when they added a layer of the tomatoes that were doing so well there. Italian pizzas vary in depth, getting thicker as you travel northwards. Pizza dough is given just one rising to produce its characteristic compact and resilient consistency.

175 G (6 OZ) UNBLEACHED STRONG WHITE FLOUR

¼ TEASPOON SALT

I TEASPOON EASY-BLEND YEAST

APPROXIMATELY 150 ML (¼ PINT) WARM WATER

I TABLESPOON OLIVE OIL

Sift the flour and salt into a bowl, stir in the yeast and form a well in the centre. Slowly pour in the warm water and the oil, stirring the dry ingredients into the liquids with your hands to make a wet dough. Beat for 2-3 minutes then turn on to a floured surface and knead for about 5 minutes or until the dough becomes smooth and elastic. Transfer to a bowl, cover with a clean cloth and leave in a warm place for about I hour until doubled in bulk.

Put the bakestone or quarry tiles, if using, in the oven to heat for 20 minutes and flour a paddle or sheet of cardboard, or oil a baking sheet.

Turn the dough on to a floured surface, knead for 2-3 minutes, then roll to a circle about 25 cm (10 inches) in diameter, making the edges slightly thicker than the centre. Carefully transfer the dough to the paddle, cardboard or baking sheet, keeping the circular shape. The pizza base is now ready to cover with your chosen topping.

Transfer the prepared pizza to the bakestone or quarry tiles, if using, and bake in a preheated oven, 220°C (425°F), Gas Mark 7, for about 20 minutes until the pizza is risen and the outside rim and base are crisp and golden.

PIZZA TOPPINGS

Roasted Red Pepper and Black Olive – I quantity pizza base. Finely chop 100 g (3½ oz) pitted black olives with ½ small onion and I clove of garlic. Slowly mix in 2 tablespoons olive oil. Add black pepper to taste then spread evenly over the pizza base, right to the edges. Scatter over 3 charred and sliced red peppers, sprinkle with 175 g (6 oz) coarsely grated mozzarella cheese and a few black olives. Sprinkle the baked pizza with torn basil and a chopped red onion.
Serves 2

Caramelized Onion, Gorgonzola and Walnut – I quantity pizza dough. Gently soften, brown and lightly caramelize 500 g (I lb) chopped and salted Spanish onions in a little unsalted butter and olive oil in a heavy frying pan. Stir in I tablespoon finely chopped rosemary, leave to cool, then spread the onions over the dough right to the edges. Sprinkle with pepper and scatter over 125 g (4 oz) chopped Gorgonzola cheese and 50 g (2 oz) chopped walnuts.
Serves 2

Artichoke and Mushroom – add a squeeze of lemon juice to the oil from 400 g (13 oz) artichokes in oil and brush over the pizza base. Slice the artichokes in half. Sauté 125 g (4 oz) sliced oyster mushrooms in olive oil, toss with the artichokes and distribute evenly over the base. Scatter over 125 g (4 oz) grated fontina cheese. Sprinkle the baked pizza with chopped marjoram.
Serves 2

Goats' Cheese, Tomato and Pesto – spread with Pesto (see page 23), cover with thinly sliced well-flavoured tomatoes, then scatter over about 150 g (5 oz) crumbled goats' cheese, trickle with virgin olive oil. Garnish the baked pizza with basil leaves, if liked.
Serves 2

GREEK SWEET EASTER BREAD

This plaited loaf with hard-boiled eggs – dyed red and polished with olive oil – nestling in it, is just one of the many sweet things that are made to celebrate a festival, in this case the ending of the 40-day Lenten fast. On the islands, the breads are the traditional gift from children to their godparents, who hang them on their walls for decoration on Easter day before eating them. In Greece, red-dyed eggs are purported to have protective powers and packets of them are sold at every pavement kiosk and general store for weeks before Easter. Similar eggs can easily be prepared by hard boiling eggs in water coloured dark red with a few drops of dark red edible food colouring.

For the finest texture, the dough should be left to rise several times. The loaf may also be decorated with blanched almonds and sesame or caraway seeds.

3 TABLESPOONS LUKEWARM WATER

150 ML (¼ PINT) LUKEWARM MILK

500 G (1 LB) STRONG PLAIN WHITE FLOUR

GRATED RIND OF 1 ORANGE

1½ TEASPOONS EASY-BLEND YEAST

OIL FOR BRUSHING

75 G (3 OZ) UNSALTED BUTTER, SOFTENED

75 G (3 OZ) CASTER SUGAR

2 EGGS, BEATEN

3 RED-DYED EGGS (SEE ABOVE)

1 BEATEN EGG YOLK FOR GLAZING

2 TABLESPOONS SPLIT ALMONDS

Add the water to the milk. Stir together the flour, orange rind and yeast in a large bowl. Mix the liquid into the dry ingredients to form a smooth dough, and then knead the dough until it is soft, pliable and elastic.

Brush a bowl with oil, place the dough in it, cover and leave at room temperature until doubled in bulk.

Turn the dough on to a lightly floured surface and knead lightly and briefly. Repeat the rising to make a loaf with a finer texture. Alternatively, you can omit the second rising.

While the dough is rising, beat together the unsalted butter and caster sugar in a bowl until creamy. Gradually beat in the eggs.

Tip the dough on to the work surface, lightly pinch in the butter mixture, then knead briefly to incorporate evenly.

Divide the dough into 3 equal pieces then roll out each piece to a long strand about the thickness of a sausage and tapered at both ends. Dampen one end of each strand and press these ends together, then plait the strands, incorporating the hard-boiled, red-dyed eggs at even intervals. Carefully transfer the loaf to an oiled baking sheet and leave until doubled in bulk.

Brush the top of the loaf with beaten egg yolk and sprinkle over the almonds. Bake in a preheated oven, 200°C (400°F), Gas Mark 6, for 30-35 minutes until golden brown on top and the bottom sounds hollow when tapped. Leave to cool on a wire rack.

Makes 1 loaf

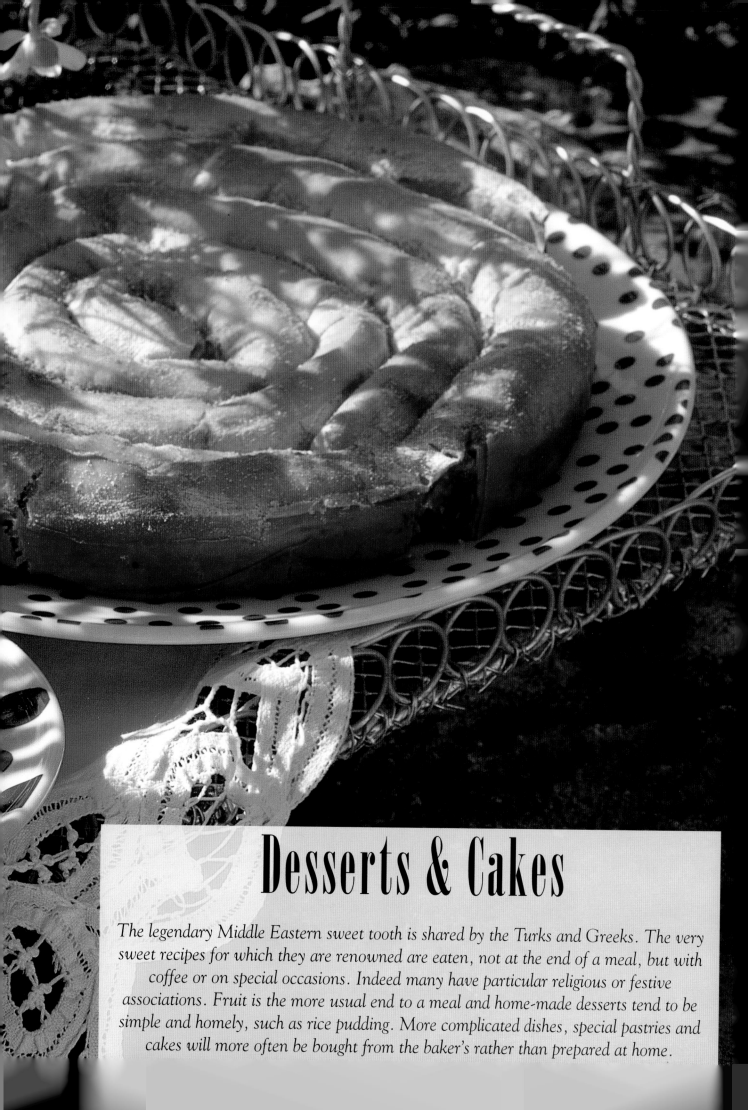

Desserts & Cakes

The legendary Middle Eastern sweet tooth is shared by the Turks and Greeks. The very sweet recipes for which they are renowned are eaten, not at the end of a meal, but with coffee or on special occasions. Indeed many have particular religious or festive associations. Fruit is the more usual end to a meal and home-made desserts tend to be simple and homely, such as rice pudding. More complicated dishes, special pastries and cakes will more often be bought from the baker's rather than prepared at home.

ALMOND PASTRY SNAKE

The Moroccan name for this rich, lightly perfumed pastry, 'M'hanncha', means 'the snake', accurately describing its coiled shape. The snake will keep for several days if stored in an airtight container in a cool place, but not the refrigerator. Reheat gently before serving, if liked.

250 G (8 OZ) GROUND ALMONDS

175 G (6 OZ) ICING SUGAR

1 EGG, SEPARATED

FEW DROPS OF ALMOND ESSENCE

1½ TABLESPOONS ROSE WATER

ICING SUGAR FOR SPRINKLING

6 SHEETS OF FILO PASTRY

4 TABLESPOONS OLIVE OIL

TO DECORATE

ICING SUGAR

GROUND CINNAMON

Stir the ground almonds and icing sugar together and mix to a paste with the egg white, almond essence and rose water. Divide into 3 equal pieces. Sift icing sugar over the work surface then roll out each piece of almond paste to a 47.5 cm (19 inch) long 'sausage', about 1 cm (½ inch) thick.

Brush a sheet of filo pastry with oil, cover with a second sheet of pastry and brush that with oil; cover the unused pastry with a damp cloth. Place one almond 'sausage' along the length of the oiled pastry, about 2.5 cm (1 inch) from the edge. Roll up the pastry, enclosing the almond 'sausage'. Form into a loose coil starting in the centre of an oiled 20 cm (8 inch) round loose-bottomed flan tin.

Repeat with the remaining almond 'sausages' and pastry. Join one to the end of the coil in the tin, continue the coil outwards, then repeat with the last piece.

Beat the egg yolk with a pinch of ground cinnamon and brush over the top. Bake in a preheated oven, 180°C (350°F), Gas Mark 4, for about 30 minutes until golden and crisp on top.

Remove the sides of the tin, carefully turn the coil over, return to the base of the tin and place in the oven for a further 10 minutes until the bottom is brown. Invert on to a cooling rack and leave to cool slightly. Sift over icing sugar and ground cinnamon. Serve warm, cut into wedges.

Makes 12 pieces

VALENCIAN CAKE

Oranges and almonds were both introduced to the Valencian area of Spain by the Arabs and are still important crops – both in the cooking and as a valuable export. The sweetness and flavour of the oranges and the freshness of the almonds will make all the difference to whether this is just a good, moist cake with a lingering orange flavour or a very special one. Pounding the nuts gives a more interesting texture, but if you feel this is too laborious, use half ground almonds and half finely chopped almonds. I recommend waiting for a day before eating the cake, as it will be even better.

125 G (4 OZ) BLANCHED ALMONDS

4 EGGS, SEPARATED

175 G (6 OZ) CASTER SUGAR

GRATED RIND AND JUICE OF 3 ORANGES

1 CINNAMON STICK, BROKEN IN HALF

1 TABLESPOON ORANGE LIQUEUR (OPTIONAL)

Butter and flour a 20 cm (8 inch) round non-stick or spring-form cake tin. Pound the almonds in a mortar using a pestle until reduced to coarse crumbs.

Whisk the egg yolks and 125 g (4 oz) of the sugar until thick, then stir in the orange rind and almonds. Using a clean whisk, whisk the egg whites until stiff but not dry. Fold one third of the egg whites into the almond mixture until just evenly mixed, then add the remaining egg whites in two batches in the same way. Spoon into the cake tin and bake in a preheated oven 180°C (350°F), Gas Mark 4, for 45 minutes until golden and set in the centre. Do not worry if the cake rises then deflates again. Leave to cool a little, then transfer to a deep serving plate.

Heat the remaining sugar in the orange juice with the cinnamon stick, stirring until the sugar has dissolved, then boil for a couple of minutes. Remove from the heat, add the liqueur, if using, then slowly pour the syrup over the entire top of the cake until it has all been absorbed.

Serves 6-8

Clockwise from right: Almond Pastry Snake, Valencian Cake and Greek Custard Pie

GREEK CUSTARD PIE

This is a lighter version of baklava. If the sweetness of this recipe is not to your liking, adjust to taste.

8 SHEETS OF FILO PASTRY

MELTED UNSALTED BUTTER FOR BRUSHING

ROSE OR ORANGE FLOWER WATER TO SERVE (OPTIONAL)

FILLING

900 ML (1½ PINTS) MILK

I CINNAMON STICK

125 G (4 OZ) SUGAR

7 TABLESPOONS FINE SEMOLINA

1½ TABLESPOONS GRATED ORANGE RIND

6 EGGS, BEATEN

SYRUP

175 G (6 OZ) SUGAR

3 TABLESPOONS LEMON JUICE

LARGE STRIP OF FINELY PARED LEMON RIND

LARGE STRIP OF FINELY PARED ORANGE RIND

To make the filling, boil the milk with the cinnamon stick, remove from the heat, cover and leave for 30 minutes. Stir in the sugar and return to the boil. Stir in the semolina and simmer gently for about 5 minutes. Remove from the heat, remove and reserve the cinnamon stick and stir in the orange rind and the eggs. Lay a sheet of dampened greaseproof paper on the surface, leave to cool completely.

Butter a 33 x 23 cm (13 x 9 inch) baking tin, line with 4 sheets of filo, brushing each with melted butter; cover remaining filo with a damp tea towel. Spread filling evenly over the filo, cover with remaining pastry, buttering each sheet first. Trim the edges, score the surface into 7 cm (3 inch) diamonds with a sharp knife. Bake in preheated oven, 180°C (350°F), Gas Mark 4, for 45-50 minutes until crisp and the filling is set. Leave to cool in the tin, on a wire rack.

To make the syrup, gently heat the sugar with the lemon juice, 250 ml (8 fl oz) water, the lemon and orange rinds and the reserved cinnamon stick, stirring until the sugar dissolves. Bring rapidly to the boil and boil for 2-3 minutes. Cover, remove from heat and leave until lukewarm. Remove the fruit rinds and cinnamon stick, slowly and carefully pour the syrup evenly over the pie and leave for the syrup to be absorbed. Serve cut into diamonds with a few drops of rose or orange flower water sprinkled over, if liked.

Serves 12

RICE PUDDING

Rice pudding is popular from Morocco to Greece – and the people in those countries really do know how to make a good rice pud (no shades of the school lunch version). They cook the rice slowly for a long time, coaxing it into absorbing plenty of milk, so making a very creamy pudding. Almonds are often added, giving more flavour. Traditionally, the nuts would be transformed into almond milk by pounding by hand, but nowadays it can be done by grinding the nuts in a blender, mixing in hot water, then straining the result. This is repeated once more. The quicker and easier way is to add freshly ground almonds to the pudding, which will make it even creamier (because extra milk is needed), give more flavour and a different texture.

APPROXIMATELY I LITRE (1¾ PINTS) MILK

50 G (2 OZ) PUDDING (SHORT GRAIN) RICE, RINSED AND DRAINED

50 G (2 OZ) SUGAR

I-1½ TABLESPOONS ORANGE FLOWER OR ROSE WATER

TO DECORATE

CHOPPED PISTACHIO NUTS OR ALMONDS

CRYSTALLIZED VIOLETS OR ROSES

Heat the milk in a heavy, preferably non-stick saucepan. Sprinkle over the rice and sugar and bring to the boil, stirring. Lower the heat and cook very gently, stirring occasionally, until the pudding is thick, velvety and falls easily from the spoon – this may take anything up to 2 hours. Use a heat diffusing mat, if necessary, to prevent the rice cooking too quickly and sticking. Stir in the orange flower water or rose water to taste.

Pour into a serving dish or individual dishes. Serve warm or cold with pistachio nuts, almonds, crystallized violets or roses scattered over.

Serves 4

PEACHES POACHED IN DESSERT WINE

A saying with much truth is that the food and wine of an area go well together. A very good example derives from the two fruits of the Languedoc soil – plump, fragrantly juicy peaches and Muscat de Lunel wine, with its luscious, delicately honeyed taste and light underlying acidity that prevents it being cloying. The combination of peaches in dessert wine works well even if the fruit and wine come from elsewhere and it is a good way of improving peaches lacking in character. The nearest substitute (in geographical as well as quality terms) for Muscat de Lunel is the more widely available Muscat de Frontignac.

25 G (1 OZ) CASTER SUGAR

300 ML (½ PINT) MUSCAT DE LUNEL OR SIMILAR DESSERT WINE

LONG STRIP OF LEMON RIND

LONG STRIP OF ORANGE RIND

4 RIPE BUT FIRM PEACHES, HALVED AND STONED

Gently heat the sugar in the wine in a frying pan that the peach halves will just fit in a single layer, stirring until dissolved. Add the lemon and orange rinds and the peaches. Add sufficient water almost to cover the peaches, then poach until tender – 5-10 minutes depending on ripeness. Using a slotted spoon, lift the peaches from the pan, remove their skins and place the fruit, cut-side up, in a shallow serving dish.

Boil the liquid until very lightly syrupy and pour over the fruit. Leave to cool, cover and place in the refrigerator for about 2 hours. For a special occasion, serve the peaches topped with Ricotta Pudding (see next recipe).

Serves 4

RICOTTA PUDDING

This is an Italian pudding, 'burdino', so would be more usually baked, but I prefer it uncooked when it is lighter and more delicate. Mascarpone is the most voluptuous cheese and, until recently, Italians managed to keep it to themselves, as it could be made only during the winter months and had to be eaten within a few days. However, now, the UHT process, which heats the cheese to a high temperature for a short time, has extended the shelf-life of the cheese and it can be made year round. The flavour does suffer a bit though, so if you are lucky enough to obtain unheat-treated cheese, snap it up.

50 G (2 OZ) MIXED CANDIED CITRON PEEL AND APRICOTS, FINELY CHOPPED

1½ TABLESPOONS BRANDY OR COINTREAU

250 G (8 OZ) FRESH RICOTTA CHEESE

2 EGGS, SEPARATED

65 G (2½ OZ) VANILLA CASTER SUGAR

FINELY GRATED RIND OF ½ LEMON

150 ML (¼ PINT) MASCARPONE CHEESE

25 G (1 OZ) AMARETTI BISCUITS, CRUSHED

RIPE PEACHES, RASPBERRIES, STRAWBERRIES OR CHERRIES TO SERVE

Leave the candied fruits to soak in the brandy or Cointreau for 30 minutes.

Sieve the ricotta into a bowl and beat in the egg yolks, sugar, lemon rind, soaked fruits and any remaining liquid. Gently fold in the mascarpone cheese.

In a clean dry bowl, whisk the egg whites until stiff but not dry, then gently fold into the ricotta mixture. Pour into a large bowl, cover and chill for 4-6 hours. Sprinkle over the amaretti just before serving with the fruit.

Serves 4

*Peaches Poached in Dessert Wine
topped with Ricotta Pudding*

Index

Author's acknowledgement

During my work on the preparation of this book many
people have helped me, some knowingly, others, such as
shop-keepers and stall-holders, unknowingly. To everyone
I extend a big thank you. To Emirates Airline and
the Dubai Hilton I offer my thanks for their
generous hospitality.

The publishers would also like to thank
the hotel, La Residencia, Mallorca
for the kind use of their facilities.